KEEP YOUR ETHICAL EDGE SHARP

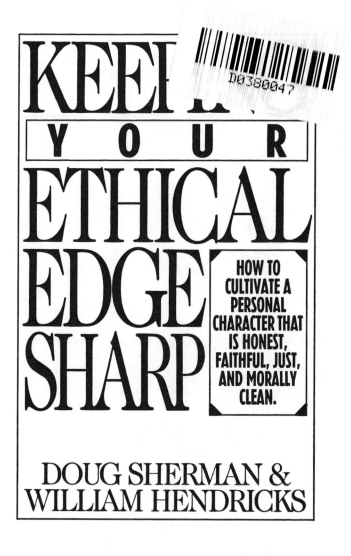

HOW TO CULTIVATE A PERSONAL CHARACTER THAT IS HONEST, FAITHFUL, JUST, AND MORALLY CLEAN.

DOUG SHERMAN & WILLIAM HENDRICKS

NAVPRESS ◑™
A MINISTRY OF THE NAVIGATORS
P.O. BOX 6000, COLORADO SPRINGS, COLORADO 80934

The Navigators is an international Christian organization. Jesus Christ gave His followers the Great Commission to go and make disciples (Matthew 28:19). The aim of The Navigators is to help fulfill that commission by multiplying laborers for Christ in every nation.

NavPress is the publishing ministry of The Navigators. NavPress publications are tools to help Christians grow. Although publications alone cannot make disciples or change lives, they can help believers learn biblical discipleship, and apply what they learn to their lives and ministries.

Library of Congress Catalog Card Number: 90-60206
ISBN 08910-92862

Third printing, 1992

Scripture quotations in this publication are from the *New American Standard Bible* (NASB), © The Lockman Foundation 1960, 1962, 1963, 1968, 1971, 1972, 1973, 1975, 1977. Other versions used include: the *Holy Bible: New International Version* (NIV), copyright © 1973, 1978, 1984, International Bible Society, used by permission of Zondervan Bible Publishers; and *The New Testament in Modern English* (PH), J.B. Phillips Translator, © J.B. Phillips 1958, 1960, 1972, used by permission of Macmillan Publishing Company.

NOTE: Throughout this book, where either the masculine or feminine pronouns are used, they should be understood as indicating both genders, unless the context implies otherwise.

Printed in the United States of America

CONTENTS

Doug Sherman is the founder and president of Career Impact Ministries (CIM), a Christian organization that helps business and professional people integrate their faith into their careers.

After graduating from the Air Force Academy with a B.S. in engineering management, Doug served as an instructor in the Advanced Jet Training Program, a position he held until he left the Air Force to attend Dallas Theological Seminary, where he received a Th.M.

Doug and his wife, Jan, live in Little Rock, Arkansas, and have three children.

William Hendricks is a writer and consultant in communication development. He received a B.A. in English literature from Harvard University, an M.S. in mass communications from Boston University, and an M.A. from Dallas Theological Seminary. He is the former vice president of CIM and a coauthor of *Rocking the Roles*.

Bill lives in Dallas, Texas, with his wife, Nancy, and their three daughters.

Other books by Doug Sherman and William Hendricks:

YOUR WORK MATTERS TO GOD (NavPress, 1987)

HOW TO BALANCE COMPETING TIME DEMANDS
(NavPress, 1989)

HOW TO SUCCEED WHERE IT REALLY COUNTS
(NavPress, 1989)

Welcome to this study of biblical integrity! As you take pains to grow in honoring Christ in your daily work and life, I trust God will honor your efforts and make you a spiritual leader where you work.

For many people, just studying the subject of integrity is not an easy task. It is common for people to think of integrity as they do politics—that theirs are better than anyone else's. But true biblical integrity comes only from a long, serious look in the mirror of God's Word. It takes a certain humility to study the topic of integrity.

Today it's possible to have mediocre integrity yet still be way ahead of "the pack." It's common for people to think of integrity as they do a light switch—either it's on or it's off. They believe that if you follow a few simple rules of conduct, you'll have integrity. Otherwise you won't.

But biblical integrity can never be fully achieved in one's lifetime. It is more like a journey in which we seek to make real progress but always have to concede that we've never arrived. Biblical integrity involves not only what we don't do, but also includes following the commands that

God has given for what we should do. It involves obeying prohibitions as well as obeying positive commands.

For some people, integrity is like a chair: if it's not comfortable, they won't use it. Biblical integrity, as you will see, involves a price. This cost pales, though, in light of the cost of compromise.

If there were ever a day for followers of Christ to study biblical integrity, this is that day! This book was written to equip and encourage you to honor Christ at work so that you will be the moral and spiritual leader He intended. No matter where you are on the path to biblical integrity, God's Word can help you take steps in the right direction.

I urge you, then, to prepare yourself to take whatever steps God will show you, and to ask Him to give you the courage to do whatever is right in His eyes, no matter what the cost may be to your reputation, career success, or financial security. For only then can you be really "free," and only then can you be Christ's disciple.

I think the highest and noblest thing any man or woman can ever do is to live for Christ in the midst of a tough, secular work world: "prove yourselves to be blameless and innocent, children of God above reproach in the midst of a crooked and perverse generation, among whom you appear as lights in the world, holding fast the word of life" (Philippians 2:15-16).

Your integrity is like the edge of a knife that is continually being blunted by the environment around you and needs to be sharpened. This book is written to help you keep it sharp!

AN ADDED BONUS

Since my days in college I have both struggled to honor Christ at work and attempted to help others do the same.

Nothing I've seen has had as much impact on lives as discussion groups. In the back of this book you will find some discussion material. You can use the content of this study with one or more people.

Maximum life change seems to occur when you're with a person in a process, over time. A discussion group can add a rich enhancement to this material as you see how others are learning to honor Christ. Such a group can also give you the encouragement and accountability you need to "make it" amid the strong pressures of the marketplace. Why not ask one or more of your peers to join you for a weekly discussion using the questions at the back of this book?

ACKNOWLEDGMENTS

It would be impossible to recall all of the many people who have had a part in producing this book. Bill and I owe a lot to our parents, Dick and Mary Lee Sherman and Howard and Jeanne Hendricks, who first instilled in us the fundamentals of right and wrong and the value of character. Later, many friends and authority figures reinforced the basics and added to them. During my days in the Air Force, I particularly benefited from the input of Captain Rich Cardiel and Brigadier General Jerry White (now general director of The Navigators).

More recently, I've appreciated the help of Terry Prindiville, Frank and Cathy Tanana, Mike Reilly, Ed Johnson, Rex Sanders, Wayne Hey, Charlie Olcott, Bob Buford, Fred Smith Jr., Jack Eckerd, Jim Roberts, Fred Laughlin, Don Meredith, Doug Coe, Doug Holladay, Ray Blunt, Ron Bower, John Isch, Bob Varney, Trey Yarbrough, Ray and Marlene Glenn, and Jean Taft.

I've also appreciated the technical support and encouragement of the NavPress publishing team: John

Eames, Bruce Nygren, Volney James, Steve Eames, and the rest of the crew. A special thanks on this one to Debby Weaver.

Another irreplaceable helper has been Karolynn Simmons, our word processor, who somehow manages to turn our Syrophoenician hieroglyphics into English! Whenever I talk about a good work ethic in this book, I could easily supply Karolynn as an outstanding example.

Finally, Bill and I need to thank the people who help keep us honest, our wives and families: Jan, Jason, Matthew, and Jennifer Sherman, and Nancy, Brittany, and Kristin Hendricks. They are the most important part of keeping our own ethical edges as sharp as possible!

ABOUT THE AUTHORS

Recall the metaphor of biblical integrity as being like a journey. Please understand that we as authors are far from having arrived. We're not perfect, we're simply inviting you and challenging ourselves to push further toward the goal of Christlikeness.

This book is a joint effort between myself as a speaker and Bill as a writer. Most of the material in this book was adapted from the messages and materials I have developed for conferences and small group discussions over the past six years. Bill has worked with me through writing and editing—tailoring this material for you. We both share the conviction of the principles contained in this book. It is dedicated to you and to the glory of God.

DOUG SHERMAN

CHAPTER ONE

"Integrity Is Nice if You Can Afford It!"

Many of us feel like we're sinking in th3 quicksand of a moral morass.

FOREIGN CARS AND FOREIGN GODS

Traffic in the Washington, D.C., area is unbearable. On a typical weekday morning, I must leave my house at 5:00 a.m. to make a 7:30 a.m. meeting in the city. And I only live twenty-five miles south, and along a major interstate highway at that. At this predawn hour a sea of cars creeps along at a snail's pace. There are people packed in vans en route to the Pentagon, there are professionals who work in the "high-tech" areas west of D.C., and there are the myriads who work for the government agencies. Foreign cars are very popular in this moving parking lot—a rather strange contrast to the patriotic career selection most have made. As I join this groggy throng, I often wonder what these people are thinking about as they head to work.

Although living in a "power center" like Washington may seem glamorous, life is not easy here. Home prices take your breath away along with all your discretionary income. Taxes make you think that only D.C. residents fund the entire national budget. And traffic is discussed in any and every gripe session. This area is home to very few. It is a revolving door of national and international leaders in government, business, education, and health care who are here for a few years, make their mark, and move on. As the *Washington Post Magazine* put it recently, no one moves to the area for the scenery. Why people put up with all the headaches voluntarily, relates to the two passions of work experienced everywhere.

The first passion is *the quest for personal significance.* I call these rewards *ego*-biscuits, because the way people pursue them reminds me of how a hungry dog will drool, leap high in the air, and perform all of his tricks over and over as long as you feed him those concrete-like dog biscuits.

We live in a work world addicted to *ego*-biscuits. People will jump with all their might for whatever the ego-biscuits are in their career. For someone in the military it might be a promotion or a medal. For the business person it's often the car or the swiss watch. For many of us it's the size of our home and the kind of clothes we wear. For educators it's professional recognition and the status of degrees. For the politicians it can be proximity to power— or rather to powerful people. The respect of peers, the boss, or even of parents qualifies as ego-biscuits too. A major motivation behind work is this addiction to ego-biscuits— which, of course, satisfy for only a short time and leave us hungry again. The applause lasts for only a while. Performance can always find an unfavorable comparison, and Bavarian status cars eventually wear out.

The second passion of work is to *improve one's life-style.* No matter how much we have, we quickly tire of it and want more. Who wouldn't want a lifestyle of more comfort and convenience? Think of the last time you were in the home of someone wealthier than you. Didn't you feel that you deserved what they had? Did you feel that *if* you could have such a nice place, you too could be happy and comfortable. We all have the disease. I'm not talking about providing for ourselves and our families; there's nothing wrong with that.

These two passions—the quest for significance and to improve one's lifestyle—combine giving career success a position of dominance whether we enjoy it or not. Actually, the issue of career achievement has risen to a position of being sacred. It is the idol of our day.

When you think of an idol, you probably think of a native in a foreign land bowing before a statue. But sociologists define an idol as anything that (1) defines a person's self-worth, (2) is the controlling center of a person's life, and (3) is the last in a series of priorities to be abandoned. The career is sacred today. This is true even for many who claim that their real god is *God.* For many Christians, Jesus Christ is simply the caboose on a train driven by career success. He is certainly in their life, but not the controlling center of it.

This whole issue has a tremendous impact on the subject of ethics and integrity. Integrity involves two issues: a study of what is the right thing to do, and consideration of what price you are willing to pay to do the right thing. Both are vital aspects of the discussion. An environment where the god of career achievement reigns provides fertile ground for ethical compromise as we will see later.

Think carefully about the following real life situations and how the issue of authority, or what god we follow, impacts decisions.

Charlie was the CEO of one of the largest franchisers in the country. Negotiations were under way to sell the firm's parent company to a foreign investor. Charlie was asked to represent the value of his company at a price considerably higher than he, in conscience, felt it was worth. To inflate the price seemed wrong, but what was his alternative? To refuse meant risking vaporizing a twenty-five-year corporate career climb, along with a hefty payoff when the deal went through.

Alicia was an administrative assistant to the vice president of a financial services company. Shortly after she started her job, the firm purchased a new system of personal computers. Each of the ten areas in the company was given its own workstation. One of Alicia's tasks was to install a word processing program on each of the computers. Several weeks later, however, a friend pointed out the licensing agreement for the software. It clearly stated that the program was for use on only one machine; copying it was illegal. Alicia wondered whether she had done something wrong. After all, she was only following orders. And at this point, what could she do? What should she do?

Oscar was a sales rep for a trucking company. Faced with strong competition, he and the other salesmen had developed an enormous bag of tricks to sign new customers. Some were blatantly illegal; Oscar shied away from those. Others were just good, clean competition; Oscar was an ace at those. But the ones Oscar really struggled with were those that were legal but pretty unethical. Like taking a customer out to dinner and ordering enough liquor to lower his defenses so he'd sign agreements. That seemed shady to Oscar, yet it was common in the industry. The customers expected it, and it would be hard to compete without it.

Hank was the superintendent on a construction job where a concrete slab was to be poured. The specifications called for an eight-inch slab, but Hank was instructed to pour it at six inches. Without asking, he knew how the substitution could be made and go unnoticed: the general contractor would pay an inspector to report the thinner slab as complying with the specs. Was Hank just doing as he was told? Or was he party to a deception? But what else could he do—lose his job?

Suppose Charlie, Alicia, Oscar, or Hank came to you for advice. What would you tell them? Better yet, suppose you were in their shoes. What would you do? How would you respond to these ethical challenges? For that matter, how do you respond day by day to the moral issues you face in your own work? For what price would you compromise your integrity?

The follower of Christ comes to the marketplace with a unique value system and style of conduct. For him, work should be an arena for serving Christ. The Bible teaches that God Himself is a Worker who meets a broad range of human needs. Man was created to be a coworker with God in all kinds of work: agriculture, medicine, business, law, and so on. Biblically, then, work is a gift from God to bring glory to Him. It is His work that we are doing every day.

If it is God's work, then it must be done His way. That's what this book is about: how to have biblical integrity in the midst of a world that does not recognize God or His laws for day-to-day living.

In this book I suggest ways that you can build a healthy, godly character. In the next few chapters, I'll describe what that looks like and why it's needed. But for now, consider a few of the benefits enjoyed by many people who have embraced the principles presented.

BENEFITS OF INTEGRITY

Self-Respect
Probably the greatest benefit of cultivating integrity is the sense of confidence and self-respect you'll feel. Having a

clear conscience, you'll sleep at night knowing that while others may have compromised to get ahead, you've remained true to what is right. You can hold your head high, secure in the knowledge that God smiles upon your character.

A Closer Walk with God
Nothing will destroy intimacy between you and God like a breach of your integrity. It will poison your fellowship and make you a stranger to the very Source of your life! By contrast, maintaining your character, especially when others around you are compromising theirs, will draw you closer to God. You'll feel His presence more keenly.

A Passion for Integrity and the Courage to Do Right
So many of us feel an "ethical loneliness" on the job, as if we're the only one with our values and convictions. As a result, we're tempted to compromise ourselves when group pressure builds. We need to develop a commitment to hold firm no matter what it costs, to value our integrity so highly that no price is too great to pay to maintain it.

Exerting Moral Leadership Where You Work
Our society is starving for moral leadership today. Nowhere is this more apparent than in the workplace. You can become a leader for moral and ethical influence where you work as you develop a Christlike character of integrity. As you live and work according to godly principles, and as you speak up to challenge others toward moral excellence, you can have a profound impact on the attitudes and behavior of coworkers.

An Effectiveness in Evangelism
Sadly, one of the major reasons nonChristians resist the gospel is because too many Christians exhibit hypocritical

compromises of integrity. By contrast, though, you can draw unbelievers to Christ as you live with genuine honesty and purity. None of us is perfect, but we can still make the gospel attractive as we show that it makes a practical difference in the way we live and work.

A Model for the Next Generation

Young people, especially our children, are so impressionable. Unfortunately, today too many of their heroes are scandalized by episodes of drug abuse, sexual immorality, and financial misdeeds. Yet the most profound and far-reaching impact on their values is the behavior they see in those who are closest to them. You could alter the course of a young person's life by the character you exhibit in your own moral choices. If you have children of your own, the most important legacy you could leave them is a reputation for integrity.

Encouragement and Restoration if You've Blown It

All of us have failed. All of us will fail. It's an unfortunate part of being human. But we can find forgiveness, and make amends where possible. Then we can move on with the conviction that it's never too late to start doing what is right.

Furthermore, we can develop Christlike compassion for others rather than self-righteous indignation over their lapses—knowing that we, too, are vulnerable. We can avoid becoming moral policemen, trying to right every wrong and imposing our morality on others. Instead, we can seek to influence others as it is most effective: from the inside.

HABITS AND DISCIPLINES TO BUILD CHARACTER

Winning the war in the area of integrity requires strategy and training. By developing a personal regimen of action and accountability, you'll toughen yourself to withstand the on-slaughts of opposing values and temptations.

As you can see, my concern is with you and your ability to confront evil as you find it. I want to avoid preachments against the multitude of forms of sin, dwelling instead on you and your character. Certainly there are many system-wide flaws in our institutions, corporations, and cultural mores that make it difficult and seemingly impossible to keep yourself clean, but that's another book. Here I want to consider how you as an individual can protect and preserve your most valuable possession: your integrity.

Let's begin, then, by surveying the ethical terrain you must traverse each day as you head for your job. It's a moral climate with which you're doubtless all too familiar—a steamy, seamy jungle where survival thrives on the ethics of expediency.

CHAPTER TWO

The Cry for
Moral Leadership

You are in hostile territory.

N ot long ago I was speaking in Canada. After concluding
my talk, the program shifted to my favorite part of any
forum, the question-and-answer period. And this group did
not disappoint me. Their questions were extremely perceptive and stimulating. One in particular I'll never forget: "We
in Canada value the leadership that the United States has
taken in the world. Yet we've been shocked by the reports of
scandal at all levels of your country, from those at the top all
the way to the bottom. What's happening? Are we just hearing the worst news, or are things really that bad?"

As an American citizen and a former military officer, my
heart sank when I heard that question. I felt a degree of
embarrassment and shame—not for my country, but for the
way its reputation has been damaged by the thoughtless,
self-seeking escapades of some people. I wanted to play the
part of an ambassador and reassure my Canadian friends
that they were hearing about only a few bad apples, that the
rest of the system has never been better.

Yet I couldn't do that. I had just completed an intensive
investigation into the morals of our country and the ethical

climate in which you and I operate, and my findings shocked me. I had to reply to the questioner, "I'm sad to say that the ethics and morality of my country are very disappointing."

So how bad is it? I think it's pretty bad—far worse than most of us realize. In this chapter, I'll document that conclusion with data from a wide variety of sources. You can decide for yourself how much our culture's values have deteriorated.

There are three reasons why I want you to go through this study on the moral temperature of the marketplace today. First, I want to establish that as a follower of Christ, you are in hostile territory ethically. Every day you work elbow to elbow with some fine people who serve a god other than yours. You should not be shocked to find that they don't acknowledge your values or support your commitment to integrity. You should, however, keep your guard up. It is all too easy to be influenced by those around you rather than to be the "influencer" that God intended. The Phillips translation of Romans 12:2 says, "Do not let the world squeeze you into its mold." We are not to let ourselves be led into moral compromise.

As a corollary to this it's important to realize that we can be more ethical than our peers—even way ahead of the "pack"—and still be ethically mediocre.

Second, I hope that there will be a certain shock value that will cause you to pound the table with your fist and say something must be done. If you ever had any doubt that God has called you to make a difference where you work—to be the moral and spiritual leader—I trust it will evaporate. You are needed desperately right now! We are in the midst of a tremendous moral mudslide, and you can help reverse the flow. I hope this study will galvanize your resolve to be ethically distinctive.

Third, I want you to get a sober estimate of our reputation in the marketplace as Christians. At a time when our culture desperately needs moral leadership, Christians are morally camouflaged. At all levels—from blue collar to gold collar—our reputation on the street is not very good. The world expects us to have high standards of integrity, and when we don't, it underscores the skepticism they have about Christ. If you were a thinking nonbeliever, and the Christians you saw daily at work took ethical shortcuts, did not pursue excellence, were weak in relationships, did not follow through with their responsibilities, then would you turn to them for answers? In our day, the work world is the proving ground for what you're made of. If Christ does not fundamentally impact our behavior at work, Christians will lose the opportunity to speak meaningfully about the Answer to life.

The church has not yet taken the marketplace seriously. Most Christians may never hear a sermon on work, read a book like this one, or study the subject of how to honor Christ by doing His work, His way. That is where you can help. Not only do you need to be a moral and spiritual leader among those outside of Christ, you also need to fulfill that role among the family of God. As I travel from coast to coast, most Christians tell me that they can't think of one other Christian in their career field whom they could look to as a model or example of excellent integrity. Maybe you are in the same boat. If so, decide today to be that model for your brothers and sisters in Christ.

IS OUR COUNTRY REALLY IN A MORAL CRISIS?

The year 1987 was a banner one for ethical scandals in the United States. The *Washington Post Magazine* dubbed it, "The Year of the Big Lie." Gary Hart, Jim and Tammy Bakker,

Iran-Contra, Ivan Boesky, Michael Deaver, the Marines in Moscow—every morning headlined a new discovery of corruption from Washington to Wall Street to Main Street. Life in the United States resembled a soap opera, so much so that Isuzu created professional liar Joe Isuzu and gained a twenty-one percent jump in sales.

In October of that year, the accounting firm Touche Ross surveyed 1,082 corporate directors and officers, business school deans, and members of Congress about matters of ethics. Ninety-four percent of respondents thought the business community was troubled by ethical problems. Thirty-three percent felt that business ethics had declined since the early 1960s.[1]

This compares with a U.S. News-CNN poll of the wider population taken at about the same time: seventy-one percent of Americans were found to be dissatisfied with levels of honesty and standards of behavior; fifty-four percent believed that people were less honest in 1987 than in 1977; only five percent felt that people had become more honest in that period.[2]

Likewise, Gallup polled Americans for the *Wall Street Journal* and found that sixty-five percent felt the overall level of ethics in our society had declined in the past decade. Only nine percent felt it had risen.[3]

When we look at comments that Touche Ross solicited from leaders in particular professions, we find the same widespread perception that ethics are in decline. Former Chief Justice Warren Burger wrote about law: "The sad truth is becoming more and more apparent [that] our profession has seen a steady decline by casting aside established traditions and canons of professional ethics that evolved over the centuries."[4]

Of government, former Senator John Tower of Texas wrote the following. (Some of Tower's words may sound incredibly ironic to you in light of accusations leveled at him during his failed bid at Secretary of Defense.)

Almost daily, the public is confronted with yet another indicator that the air of American politics is tainted with the smell of corruption—or at least of questionable ethics. . . . Increasingly, political observers now argue that the American public's confidence in its leaders and institutions is so shaken that our entire system of government has been undermined. . . .
It is imperative that those who serve the public interest be held to higher standards of ethics, morality, and accountability than any others. However, while instances of true corruption are extremely disturbing and must be prosecuted to the extent of the law, equally troublesome is the increasing trend toward a political climate where candidates and public servants are judged less on the quality of their views and commitment to issues of public policy than on whether they have lived their entire lives free of blemish.[5]

Kenneth Blanchard, author of the *One-Minute Manager* and *The Power of Ethical Management,* observed,

All across our country, there is evidence of a deterioration of ethics. Nowhere is this decline greater than in the world of business. . . . [I]ndividuals seemingly have come to check their values at the door when they enter the office. The attitude in many businesses appears to be profit at any cost, especially if a company's gains can be at the expense of a competitor—and, sometimes, even if it is at the expense of its customers.[6]

Can business schools help? Not much, according to those who teach there. "If people think we can take a person 23 to 26 years old and within two years totally retool them, they're wrong," says Russell Palmer, dean of the prestigious Warton School at the University of Pennsylvania. "Putting the entire focus on business schools is ridiculous."[7]

MIT's Lester Thurow agrees:

> Business students come to us from our society. If they haven't been taught ethics by their families, their clergymen, their elementary and secondary schools, their liberal arts colleges or engineering schools or the business firms where most of them have already worked prior to getting a business degree, there is very little we can do.
>
> Injunctions to "be good" don't sway young men and women in their mid-to-late '20s. In the final analysis, what we produce is no worse than what we get.[8]

ETHICAL SCORECARDS

So much for opinion. What are the facts? Are moral and ethical lapses in today's workplace relatively major and widespread, or only minor and infrequent? Consider several categories.

Executive Ethics

Both experts and laypeople agree that the moral tone for any organization is set by those at the top. Seventy-three percent of the Touche Ross respondents named the CEO as playing the biggest role. Others mentioned included an employee's immediate supervisor and the company's board of directors.[9]

A study of executives "indicated that the ethical standards of upper level executives often serve as models for lower level executives."[10]

So what sort of behavior do such influential executives practice? In a landmark survey for the *Wall Street Journal* in 1983, Gallup found some rather startling disparities between executives and the general public. Eighty percent of executives poled admitted to having driven while drunk, compared with thirty-three percent of the general population. Seventy-eight percent had used the company phone for personal long distance calls. Thirty-five percent had overstated deductions on tax forms. And three out of four had pilfered work supplies for personal use, as opposed to forty percent of the general public.[11]

As for executive ethics in business itself, white-collar crime steals at least $40 billion a year from the companies, governments, and individuals that make up the United States' economy.[12] By the way, that's a full one percent bite out of the gross national product, and ten times the cost of street crime.

Employee Theft

There are many ways for employees to steal from their companies. The former head of a major drug store chain told me that ten years ago, he estimated pilferage in the retail sector at two percent of total sales. Today he believes it is four percent.

That squares with a comment I heard from an executive in the food service industry. Employee theft there is generally considered to be three percent of sales. These losses are substantial when you consider that most retail operations live on a thin margin of profit, and do well if they clear six or seven percent of gross sales. Worst of all, this loss is due to theft by an employer's own people.

Another kind of theft is time theft: excessively long

lunch breaks, late arrivals and early departures, shooting the breeze by the water cooler, or the worst, unauthorized absenteeism (calling in sick when not sick). One international recruiting firm puts the cost of shirking work at $100 billion to $150 billion a year. Other studies estimate it to be as high as $350 billion!

Is that figure possible? Well, consider the fact that General Motors routinely loses nine percent of employee payroll hours to unauthorized absenteeism—about $1 billion a year. (Think about that the next time you buy a car!) In 1987, GM had to shut down operations at its Pontiac East assembly plant for two days at the start of hunting season![13]

General Motors is not alone. On any given day, one million workers are no-shows—many for unauthorized reasons. Nearly one-third of Americans have at some point called in sick when not sick.[14] This is a major concern when we think of the loss of productivity that weakens our competitive posture in a tough, global economy.

Another way to steal from employers is to dial long distance at the company's expense. A study by the Office of Technology Assessment determined that a third of all calls paid for by the Federal Government were of a personal nature, costing Uncle Sam more than $100 million a year.[15] Imagine if this same percentage applied to your company!

No wonder call accounting has become one of the fastest growing segments of the telecommunications industry. Employers are eager to use electronic means to staunch a tidal wave of "phone theft." In 1985, 25,000 companies used such services. In just three years, the figure more than doubled to 63,000.

Dishonesty

So pervasive has lying become that in 1987, the *Washington Post Magazine* decided to poll 513 randomly selected adults in the Washington, D.C., area to ask them about deception. As one might expect, the results make interesting and entertaining reading.

For example, seventy-eight percent said that the average person is basically honest. Yet ninety-two percent admitted to having told a lie. (I wonder, in light of this, can the other eight percent be trusted?) Forty-three percent admitted to having told a "serious lie," and nearly the same percentage feel that most people seriously lie a great deal or at least a fair amount.

Apparently one lie leads to another: Fifty-eight percent said that when people are caught in a lie, they frequently tell another lie to cover up.[16]

So much for Washingtonians. What about the rest of the country? A congressional subcommittee estimated that a third of all workers are hired with educational or career credentials that have been falsified in some way.[17] Similarly, Ward Howell International, Inc., found that "more than one out of four executives reported that within the previous year their organizations had hired employees 'whose job qualifications, educational credentials or salary history [had] been misrepresented.'"[18]

I call that the Joseph Biden syndrome. During Senator Biden's 1987 bid to win his party's nomination for the presidency, the candidate claimed to have attended law school on a full academic scholarship, that he'd finished in the top half of his class, that he was the "outstanding student in the political science department," and that he'd graduated with three degrees.

It didn't take the press long to check out these impressive claims. What they found earned him an award for the "best concoction of bogus academic credentials": "Biden received a half scholarship based on need; he finished seventy-sixth out of eighty-five in the class; he didn't win the outstanding political science award; and he received only one degree."[19]

Of course, lying extends to far more than overstating credentials. Perhaps you read about the *Reader's Digest* sting in the spring of 1987. Two hundred and twenty-six garages were randomly selected to repair a car with a spark plug wire pulled loose. Seventy-four percent of the garages "fixed" the car, charging as much as $500 for work not done or not needed.

Sexual Immorality
Sexual immorality may seem irrelevant to a discussion of workplace ethics. There's a popular conception among many people that "what you do on your own time is your own business and nobody else's"—certainly not your employer's. Yet the research shows an indisputable link between sexual ethics and their performance at work.

In fact, Barbara Gutek, professor of psychology at the Claremont Graduate School, writes, "I have found sex at work a problem for up to half of all workers."[20] She claims that fifty percent of all workers report having been associated with some kind of "socio-sexual experience," such as jokes, staring, or posters, and that as many as thirty-five million workers will have such an experience in any given week.

WHO ARE WE TALKING ABOUT?

I could fill an entire book with more statistics like these. But I think the point is clear: Our culture is in the midst of a moral mudslide on an unprecedented scale.

However, as one sifts through the research, it's interesting to observe the tendency for people to claim that it's "others" who are causing all the trouble or at least most of it—not them. For example, numerous studies "tend to show that business executives usually believe that they are more ethical than their peers and colleagues. While believing that they themselves are fairly ethical, there appears to be a cynicism concerning the ethical behavior of other executives."[21]

Likewise, in the Touche Ross study—undertaken at a time when publicity over ethics was at its height—a majority of business leaders in almost all industry groups said that they did not feel the public outcry over sagging ethics was overblown. The sole voices of dissent came from leaders in the aerospace and defense industries.[22] Not surprising when you consider that at the time forty-five of the nation's one-hundred-largest military contractors were under criminal investigation for kickbacks, illegal overcharges, and other sins.[23]

In short, it's always easier to point out the failures of others than to observe and correct our own. At this point a stiff challenge needs to be addressed to those of us who label ourselves "Christians." For what we'd like to believe is simply not true: that it's the rest of society acting immorally— all those pagans, those people who do not believe in Christ. They're the problem, we like to tell ourselves. But that just isn't true!

THE INTEGRITY OF CHRISTIANS

A growing body of research suggests that religious beliefs and convictions make little difference in the behavior of people on the job. For example, Gallup found that "those who attend church or synagogue or feel a religious affiliation appear only slightly more likely to walk the straight and narrow than their less pious compatriots. For instance, forty-three percent of those who don't attend religious services say they have taken home work supplies—but so do thirty-seven percent of the churchgoers."[24]

While thirty-seven percent of the unchurched report calling in sick when not sick, so do twenty-seven percent of the churched. Seventeen percent of the unchurched use the company phone for personal long distance calls, but so do thirteen percent of the churched.[25] So it goes in other categories such as overstating deductions and understating income on tax forms, overstating qualifications on résumés, looking the other way when coworkers pilfer, and so on.

Gallup concludes,

> These findings . . . show little difference in the ethical views and behavior of the churched and the unchurched, [and] will come as a shock to religious leaders to channel the new religious interest in America not simply into religious *involvement* but into deep spiritual commitment.[26]

In the Touche Ross survey, subjects were asked to rank the three groups that have been most helpful in improving business ethics: "Respondents identified business people themselves, business associations, and the courts, ranked in that order. Academism failed to place among the top three, as did government and the media, both of which rated much less helpful than academism."[27] It's interesting that churches and religion were not even mentioned.

Have churches become irrelevant on work issues? That's the conclusion of recent Gallup polls on the impact of religion in American life. In 1957, a mere fourteen percent saw religion as losing its influence; in 1988, the figure had grown to forty-nine percent. Likewise, while eighty-one percent of Americans believed that religion could answer "today's problems" in 1957, only fifty-seven percent believe that now. By contrast, the hard-core skeptics who believe religion is out of date have grown from seven percent in 1957 to a full twenty percent today![28]

When I present data such as the Gallup report, I'm often asked, "But who are these researchers measuring? Are the people *really* Christians?" The assumption is that "real" Christians don't violate ethical standards—at least not as much as "real" nonChristians.

I wish I could say that's true. But as I travel extensively and read widely and hear frequently from friends in a variety of work settings, I cannot agree that Christians—"true" Christians—in our society are better behaved ethically at work than their nonChristian coworkers. They—that is, *we*—ought to be. We have the spiritual resources to be. But the sad reality is, with few exceptions, we aren't.

As a result, we are not impressing our society that our faith has many answers for life. George Barna of the Barna Research Group makes a startling observation when he writes,

> *Fact:* Since 1980, there has been *no growth* in the proportion of the adult population that can be classified as "born again" Christians. (These are people who have made a personal commitment to Jesus Christ, accepting Him as their Lord and Savior.) The proportion of born again Christians has remained constant . . . despite the fact that churches and parachurch organizations have spent several billion dollars on evangelism. More than 10,000 hours of evangelistic television programing have been broad-cast, in excess of 5,000 new Christian books have been published, and more than 1,000 radio stations carry Christian broadcasting. And yet, despite such widespread opportunities for exposure to the

gospel, there has been no discernible growth in the size of the Christian Body.[29]

Freddie Gage, a Southern Baptist evangelist, agrees. Addressing a pastors' conference of 14,500, he said that the denomination's research department reported a drop in new converts from 363,124 in 1986, to 338,495 in 1987. That's troubling enough, but Gage pointed out that the figures were worse than they appeared because 181,000 of those baptisms were of children who grew up in Southern Baptist homes. Another 55,000 were transplants from other denominations, and 26,000 were re-baptisms of Southern Baptists who claimed their first baptisms were not genuine. That left 77,000 conversions of people from outside the Christian faith. He concluded,

> When we wash it all down, with 15 million Southern Baptists and $19 billion in property and buildings, with all our evangelistic crusades, home missionary projects, evangelism and Bible conferences, we only reached 77,000 in this lost, dying, perishing America.[30]

That's a chilling statistic! I view the Southern Baptist Convention (SBC) as far and away the most aggressive and effective of the major denominations in evangelizing new converts. But if the nation's largest denomination—an organization valued at $19 billion in property alone—was able to baptize only 77,000 brand new converts in 1987, one has to wonder whether the Christian Church as a whole is making much of an impact in our society.

Nineteen billion dollars! That's $250,000 of church assets per convert. Fifteen million members! That's about one convert for every 195 church goers. And remember, the SBC has the best track record for conversions among the major denominations. It seems that the church in America is not having much impact today. In my opinion, its position will continue to decline drastically, until it takes the person in the marketplace seriously.

THE REAL TRAGEDY

Surely this is a dark day for Christianity, at least in our society. This is not a time when we as believers should be patting ourselves on the back in any way. Yes, there are some exciting exceptions—individuals and organizations that are very impressive in their testimony—but on the whole, Christianity is at best ignored and at worst scorned when it comes to the workplace.

What a tragedy! Christ intended His followers to be "salt" and "light": the influencers in the culture, not the influenced. I believe the workplace has become our most strategic arena for influence today. Yet we find many believers who are unbelievably compromised, such that they have no impact on others for the cause of Christ. They are morally camouflaged; their faith makes not the slightest difference in their attitude or conduct in the workplace.

That's particularly tragic because God intended work as one of our greatest means toward worshiping and loving Him. Work is not a curse, as some believe. It is a gift from God through which we can serve the legitimate needs of others, meet our own needs, and express our skills and abilities to the glory of God.[31]

If we compromise our integrity on the job and violate God's standards of honesty, justice, and equity, then we violate God's gift of work and dishonor Him. In effect, we turn something that God intended for good into an instrument of evil.

Well, of course, we can always point the finger at others

and lament their failures. But what about you and me as individuals? Do we want to choose a different path, a different lifestyle and "workstyle," a character so unique and distinctive that coworkers will want to know why? In the midst of the moral mudslide all around us, do we want to stand firm for God?

I know I do! And I pray you do as well. If so, I invite you to turn with me to a discussion of how we can keep our ethical edge sharp. Let's begin with a study of integrity—your most valuable possession.

NOTES: 1. Touche Ross & Co., "Ethics in American Business: A Special Report," page 68.
2. *U.S. News & World Report,* "A U.S. News Poll: Echoes of Watergate," February 23, 1987, pages 56-57.
3. Roger Ricklefs, "Executives and General Public Say Ethical Behavior Is Declining in U.S.," *Wall Street Journal,* October 31, 1983, page 33.
4. Warren Burger quoted in Touche Ross, page 10.
5. John Tower quoted in Touche Ross, page 19.
6. Kenneth Blanchard quoted in Touche Ross, page 37.
7. Russell Palmer quoted by Sallie Gaines, "Teaching Ethics: Uproar Makes B-Schools Bristle," *Chicago Tribune,* May 17, 1987, page C-1.
8. Lester C. Thurow, "Ethics Doesn't Start in Business Schools," *New York Times,* June 14, 1987, section 4, page E25.
9. Touche Ross, page 69.
10. Newstrom and Ruch (1975), cited in Scott J. Vitell and Troy A. Festervand, "Business Ethics: Conflicts, Practices and Beliefs of Industrial Executives," *Journal of Business Ethics,* vol. 6 (1987), page 113; see pages 111-122.
11. *Wall Street Journal,* October 31, 1983, page 33.
12. Stephen Koepp, "Having It All, Then Throwing It All Away," *Time,* May 25, 1987, page 23.
13. Richard Greene, "Money For Nothing," *Forbes,* January 25, 1988, page 48.
14. *Wall Street Journal,* October 31, 1983, page 33.
15. Jeffrey Rothfeder, "Memo to Workers: Don't Phone Home," *Business Week,* January 25, 1988, pages 88-90.
16. Richard Morin, "Lies, Damn Lies and Statistics," *Washington Post Magazine,* December 27, 1987, pages 24-25.
17. *U.S. News & World Report,* page 54.

18. *U.S. News & World Report,* page 59.
19. Peter Carlson, "The Academy Awards of Untruth," *Washington Post Magazine,* December 27, 1987, page 32.
20. Barbara Gutek, *Sex and the Workplace* (San Francisco, Calif.: Jossey-Bass Publishers, 1985), page vii.
21. Vitell and Festervand, page 117.
22. Touche Ross, page 68.
23. Robert Reich, "On the Brink of an Anti-Business Era," *New York Times,* April 12, 1987, section 3, page F3.
24. Ricklefs, page 41.
25. PRRC *Emerging Trends,* "Ethics Behavior Seen Declining," vol. 5, no. 10 (December 1983), page 5.
26. PRRC *Emerging Trends,* page 5.
27. Touche Ross, page 69.
28. PPRC *Emerging Trends,* "Many More Today Than in 1986 See Religion Losing Impact on U.S. Life" (Spring 1988), page 3.
29. George Barna, *Marketing the Church* (Colorado Springs, Colo.: NavPress, 1988), pages 21-22.
30. Freddie Gage quoted by Jim Jones, "Minister Decries Drop in Baptist Convert Rate," *Fort Worth Star Telegram,* June 13, 1988, section 1, page 12.
31. For a comprehensive discussion of the idea that work is intrinsically good and the implications of that truth, see our book *Your Work Matters to God* (NavPress, 1987).

CHAPTER THREE

Integrity: Your Most Valuable Possession

*No price is too great to pay
to hold on to your integrity!*

Suppose I came to your house and offered you two or three candy bars for it. Would you trade? Obviously not! You wouldn't trade your home for a handful of candy bars, no matter how great a salesman I might be.

Yet every day people trade away something even more valuable than their homes for what amounts to candy bars by comparison. I'm thinking of the moral compromises that people make in order to gain advantage in some relatively insignificant way.

We looked at many of those compromises in the last chapter. The sad reality is that they are terribly poor bargains: something very precious squandered on something of slight worth by comparison. You see, biblically, your integrity is your most valuable asset. As Proverbs 22:1 says, "A good name is to be more desired than great riches, favor is better than silver and gold." The "good name" here has to do with a reputation for honesty and integrity, and the "favor" has to do with favor before God. Psalm 37:16 puts it this way: "Better is the little of the righteous than the abundance of many wicked."

The overwhelming teaching of Scripture is that integrity is a treasure worth paying any price to preserve—*any price*, whether it be your job, career, reputation, savings, position, whatever. I can say this unequivocally, because integrity is a value that is rooted in the very character of God.

BE HOLY!

In 1 Peter 1:14-16 we read,

> As obedient children, do not be conformed to the former lusts which were yours in your ignorance, but like the Holy One who called you, be holy yourselves also in all your behavior; because it is written, "You shall be holy, for I am holy."

This passage tells us that if we intend to identify ourselves as God's people—as His "obedient children" as verse 14 says—then our character and behavior must match His character and behavior. Our morality must square with His morality. As He is holy, so we must be holy.

I don't know how you understand the term *holy*. For many, the word conjures up images of stained glass, incense, organ music, and chanting. For others, it recalls a harsh, vindictive task master who capriciously punishes the slightest infraction, and broods over evils real and imagined. But as we examine the text of Scripture, we find a much different idea. The word we translate as *holy* comes from a Hebrew term that means "to set apart." Let me illustrate.

When Jan and I were newly married, our first dispute was over the dreaded topic of *the fine china!* The discussion went like this: First Jan began to explain to me why the china we had was not *fine* china. Certainly it was an upgrade from what I'd had as a single. In those days I used plastic dishes that I think I rescued from a dumpster or somewhere. At any rate, it worked for me.

Then when we were married, our friends and relatives gave us wedding presents, including some really nice china. But as attractive as that china was, Jan argued, it was just everyday china, not *fine* china. That would not do, she said, for when we had guests over; we had to have *fine* china.

Being the reasonable man that I am, I said, "Fine, let's get fine china. How much is it?" When I heard the price, I staggered! Did we really need such valuable dishes for those rare and special occasions when perhaps someone would come over and we would entertain in our home? Yes, she answered, because when someone comes over, we want to show them how special they are to us. And one way we show that is to bring out the fine china for the occasion. Somehow I lost the argument, and we ended up with *fine* china!

When the Bible uses the term *holy* (or its related term, *sanctified*), it describes something like fine china. If something is called "holy," that means it is set apart, either because it has extraordinary value, or because it's intended for some extraordinarily special purpose. It's not something you abuse or handle carelessly.

In the 1 Peter passage, God says that He is holy. As I've investigated that throughout Scripture, I've found that it means God is pure and morally perfect, with a purity beyond any conception that we have. He is "set apart" in the sense that He is removed from sin or evil; He is morally flawless. Therefore, He is the ultimate, perfect standard of right and wrong.

The passage is not just describing the character God has, but points out the character that you and I ought to have if we're His children: "*You* shall be holy, for I am holy." In whatever we do, we should pursue holiness—moral purity like God's. We are to be like fine china, for as God's children, we are "set apart" for a special purpose: namely, to glorify God, to live in such a way that we honor Him, love Him, and enjoy Him with all that we are and have.

I don't know what your purpose is in going to work each day. But if you intend to honor God in your work, your character should reflect the very character of God. You should be morally distinctive; you should be holy, set apart. In fact, you should stand out, because as we saw in the last chapter, most of those around you have chosen to leave God at home when they go to work. As a result, they are easily compromised when the pressure is on.

What an opportunity, then, for us as God's people to shine like stars in the darkest of nights! Philippians 2:14-15 (NIV) exhorts us to this very thing:

> Do everything without complaining or arguing, so that you may become blameless and pure, children of God without fault in a crooked and depraved generation, in which you shine like stars in the universe.

Do you shine like a star where you work? Not just in your performance and achievements, but as a moral agent? Are you blameless and pure, without fault? None of us is perfect, yet the clear point of this passage—along with the 1 Peter passage—is that we're to pursue the same moral purity that characterizes God Himself. That's pretty exacting! It doesn't leave any room for tolerance. Perfection is, after all, perfection. But the point is that when it comes to right and wrong, there are no small issues. We as humans tend to rank various sins. Even our laws distinguish between misdemeanors and felonies. But viewed from the standpoint of God's matchless perfection and holiness, sin is sin while pure means completely pure. There are no "little sins" and "big sins," just as there are no "little goods" and "big goods." Whatever we do either takes us toward or away from God.

Because sin is sin, it's so important that we not ignore even the slightest sins in our lives. To be sure, we cannot arrive at perfection overnight. But we dare not trivialize any breach of integrity as if it doesn't matter, for to do so is to invite that evil to grow. It's like a virus or cancer: It may start as a single cell, but given time, and without appropriate treatment, it can take over an entire person and ravage and kill him. As a Chinese proverb puts it, "Sow a thought, reap an action. Sow an action, reap a habit. Sow a habit, reap a destiny."

Your integrity is a valuable possession! So valuable, in fact, that God paid a tremendous price—the greatest price that ever has been or ever could be paid—to make it possible for you to share in His holiness. First Peter 1:17-19 goes on to say,

> And if you address as Father the One who impartially judges according to each man's work, conduct yourselves in fear during the time of your stay upon earth; knowing that you were not redeemed with perishable things like silver or gold from your futile way of life inherited from your forefathers, but with precious blood, as of a lamb unblemished and spotless, the blood of Christh.

If God could have done anything more to purchase your salvation from sin, He would have. But He gave all He had when He gave Christ, the Holy God who gave up His own life on behalf of unholy people. Not only should you pursue moral purity because God is pure, and because you're set apart from those who do not know God, but also out of gratitude for the selfless love that Christ extended on your behalf. Moral purity is not just something you *have to* have; it's something you *get to* have because of Christ.

WHAT IS INTEGRITY?

To summarize: Because God is holy, and because we're His children, we are to pursue a holy character and lifestyle. In practical terms, we're to live with *integrity*.

What does that mean? *Integrity*, like holy, is a word that is often used but not always understood. In the business world, people say they do business with integrity, meaning they're basically honest and give you what you pay for. At other times, a person stands for some moral principle, and we say she has integrity, meaning she has the courage of her convictions. Again, we may hear someone slander an acquaintance of ours, and we rush to defend their integrity, as we put it, meaning that we're preserving their honor and reputation.

Certainly, these ideas are all related to the concept of integrity. But at its core, integrity refers to the soundness and authenticity of something or someone. If you have integrity, it means you're for real: You're not pretending to be anything other than what you really are; you're the genuine item. Furthermore, what you are is what you're supposed to be, particularly in terms of your ethics and morals. If someone examines you carefully, they'll find you to be clean as a whistle.

This concept of integrity lies in sharp contrast to the way many people view integrity. For them, integrity refers to a short list of what they *won't* do. But biblical integrity is more than just a list of don'ts. It involves some prohibitions, but it also involves a much larger body of values concerned with what we *should* do: show love to our coworkers, be trustworthy to our employer, be honest with our customers, etc. There are far more dos than don'ts when it comes to biblical integrity.

That's why understanding integrity can't be done in just a short study. It's something we need to come back to again and again throughout our whole lives. We must continually refine and sharpen our ethical edge, or it will become dull and ineffective.

This concept of integrity fits perfectly with what we've seen in 1 Peter 1 about holiness and in Philippians 2 about shining like stars in the midst of moral darkness. If you're a person of integrity, you'll be like fine china: set apart for a special purpose. When people look closely, they'll find that you're genuine, not a hypocrite who swears allegiance to one set of values on Sunday, but lives by a completely different set of values come Monday.

Furthermore, you'll stand out in your workplace! If you're solid in your moral conduct, you'll distinguish yourself, because so many around you are settling for compromise. You'll appear like the star you're supposed to be, pouring forth the light of Christ, no matter how dark and evil the situation around you becomes. In fact, a lifestyle of integrity will have a profound *impact* where you work. Let's consider that in more detail.

THE IMPACT OF INTEGRITY

If our society needs anything today, it desperately needs moral leadership. Notice that I did not say more moralists, nor did I say we need more preachers. No, we need moral leadership, the kind of influence that comes from men and women of moral integrity who know how to live in the real world.

If you and I were to act with Christlike integrity in the

way we conduct our business, treat our customers, handle loans, deal with supervisors, approach work projects and assignments, account for our expenses, hours, and income, we could do so much to transform our workplaces! Consider the many results of having unimpeachable integrity.

Impact on Ourselves

There are numerous benefits to ourselves when we live with integrity. One I want to highlight is the sense of dignity and self-respect we feel when our lives are clean. Conversely, we feel guilt and lose self-regard when we compromise.

When I was an instructor in the Air Force, a particular colonel and I had a running battle over when students should be permitted to fly solo. The issue was largely one of money.

Obviously training pilots to fly supersonic aircraft was a costly proposition. The way the colonel saw it, the fewer rides it took to prepare a pilot, the better. It would make him look good as a commander who could get the job done in shorter time at less cost. I agreed, but I also felt that safety should override any consideration of cost. I had a few students who, even after ten flights, were not ready to go solo. So in conscience, I refused to sign them off. It was too dangerous. But the colonel would override me.

For years we went back and forth on this issue. The day when I was getting out of the service, I went to him to say good-bye. Despite our dispute over this issue, we were actually good friends, so I challenged him: "How is it that you felt okay about sending students solo, despite the extreme risk involved, only to save money and enhance your career?"

At that he looked down at his feet and replied, "Doug, I'd rather be a live coward than a dead hero." What an incredible statement of a person who has lost self-respect and courage because he has compromised his integrity!

By contrast, Proverbs 10:9 says, "He who walks in integrity walks securely." That person has a sense of confidence because he knows he is living the way he should.

Impact on Our Families

So often people think that their morality is their own, personal business, and that it has no impact on others. That's such a mistake! Everything we do is freighted with significance for how it affects others. Nowhere is the effect of our moral choices felt more than in our families.

A father took his son with him to a body shop. The man had had a fender bender and needed minor body work done. At the shop he showed the damage to the owner, and they talked awhile about what it would take to fix it. Then he produced some insurance forms and began to talk price.

"How much is your deductible?" the body shop owner asked.

"Two hundred and fifty," the man replied.

"Well, I figure this will take about two hundred and fifty dollars of repair work. So we'll put down five hundred." The repairman signed the form and handed it back. The two men shook hands, and the father and son got back in the car.

On the way home, the boy said to his dad, "I don't understand why the man put down five hundred if it's going to take only two hundred and fifty dollars to fix the car."

The father grinned and explained what had happened to his son: "Our deductible is two-fifty, which means I'd have to pay that much if we just wrote down two-fifty. But by writing five hundred, I don't have any out-of-pocket expenses, the body shop gets paid, and everyone's happy. It's the way you do these things."

Can you imagine the impact of that incident on the moral formation of that boy? He'll *never* forget that! What's worse, who knows how that lesson in ethics will carry over later to the way he takes tests in high school or college, accounts for expenses, completes his tax reports, fills orders for customers, or the way he decides a hundred other ethical decisions he'll face! As Proverbs 15:27 states, "He who profits illicitly troubles his own house." By contrast, Proverbs 20:7 says, "A righteous man who walks in his integrity—how blessed are his sons after him."

Impact on People Around Us

A life of integrity can have a profound influence on others. One benefit it creates is a moral climate in which others will be inspired to do the right thing.

A friend of mine is a salesman who travels frequently. He was once invited to join several other salesmen in his company for a special weekend with the vice president of marketing. The group had a number of sessions together, discussing the company, its sales, and related matters.

On Saturday evening, the men enjoyed a lavish dinner, and the atmosphere became relaxed and jovial. At the end of the dinner, several of the men decided to go to a movie and invited my friend "John" to join them.

At first John thought he would go with them. But when they got to the theater, he realized that they were going to see an X-rated porno film. He wanted no part of that. He'd already determined that as a believer he would not participate in such a thing. So he told the group that he was heading back to the hotel. Naturally, the others wanted to know why, so he told them: "I don't go to this kind of movie." Well, the group began to tease him and try to get him to go along, but he stood his ground, and finally walked away.

He felt lonely and even a bit embarrassed. Yet he also knew that he'd done the right thing before the Lord, and that gave him a lot of confidence.

Suddenly he heard footsteps behind him, and he turned to see one of the other salesmen hurrying to catch up. The other man said, "John, you're a Christian, aren't you?"

"Yeah, I am," replied John. "How did you know?"

"Because of the way you stood your ground back there, I just knew you had to be. You see, I'm a Christian, too. But I didn't have the guts to say no to the others about that movie—at least, not until you spoke up. Then I knew I had to leave. Thanks for saying what you did!"

John inspired moral excellence in that other believer. And even though he didn't affect the choice of the others in that situation, he still had an effect on them, if only by showing them that not everyone goes along with such behavior.

You can be like John. Your life can be so ethically distinctive that it inspires others to do what is right—even those who are unbelievers. This was Jesus' exhortation in Matthew 5:16: "Let your light shine before men in such a way that they may see your good works, and glorify your Father who is in heaven."

Impact on Our Workplace

As we saw in the example of John, a believer can profoundly affect the behavior of others by the way he behaves. Imagine, then, the impact you could have on the moral climate where you work!

Think, for instance, of the positive impact you might be able to have on the way decisions are made. In today's workplace, decisions are often made by many people providing many levels of input. As you offer your comments and interact with others, you can steer things in a positive direction. You can speak up for what is right, decent, and honest; you can mention the needs and rights of others; you can point out possible illegalities or questionable ethics.

Furthermore, you can do all of this without acting like a moral policeman. In fact, you do not necessarily have to bring in Scripture or preach a sermon to get your points across. As a member of the team, you have a voice in the decisions, and you can use that as an opportunity to influence your company toward positive values. As a believer, you have a responsibility to do so.

Obviously you'll never make your company perfect or clear out all the evils you see around you. But it's amazing how differently companies are run when believers use their positions of influence to affect the ethical climate in which the business operates.

Impact on Our Relationship with God

It's obvious that God values integrity. So it makes sense that those who want to enjoy a close, intimate relationship with Him must become people of integrity. This is the point of Psalm 15 (NIV), which begins by asking, "LORD, who may dwell in your sanctuary? Who may live on your holy hill?" (verse 1). In other words, who gets to be close to God? The answer is clear (verse 2): "He whose walk is blameless."

The word *blameless* reinforces the concept of integrity. It's the idea of a flawless piece of china, a valuable quality of life, a life that is morally pure. Psalm 15 tells us that if we want to know God intimately, then we must pursue a pure lifestyle. The rest of the passage spells out what a blameless lifestyle looks like (verses 2-5, NIV):

> He whose walk is blameless
>   and who does what is righteous,
> who speaks the truth from his heart
>   and has no slander on his tongue,

who does his neighbor no wrong
and casts no slur on his fellow man,
who despises a vile man
but honors those who fear the LORD,
who keeps his oath
even when it hurts,
who lends his money without usury
and does not accept a bribe against the innocent.
He who does these things
will never be shaken.

Impact on the Cause of Christ

I've already described the devastating impact that widespread moral compromise among Christians today is having on the advance of the gospel. While people in our society are still coming to faith, they are not doing so at a rate that keeps pace with the growth of the population. I believe that one of the main reasons for this evangelistic stagnation is the loss of integrity on the part of so many believers at their jobs.

Yet the workplace is probably the most strategic arena for Christian thinking and influence today. Nowhere else will your unbelieving coworkers have such an opportunity to see genuine Christianity up close than when they are around you. That's why Titus 2:9-10 (NIV) says,

Teach slaves to be subject to their masters in everything, to try to please them, not to talk back to them, and not to steal from them, but to show that they can be fully trusted, so that in every way they will make the teaching about God our Savior attractive.

Are you making the gospel attractive to those with whom you work? Can they see Jesus in the way you treat them? Is there a difference in your ethics and values, a distinctive, Christlike quality in the way you conduct business? Is your speech pure? Are your decisions clean? Is your reputation above reproach?

It may seem that I'm preaching perfection here. I'm not, but I am concerned that people find salvation in Christ. I would never want someone to reject Christ because I lived a life of duplicity, or because my reputation was so compromised that I could not speak for Christ with any credibility.

How about you? Are your lifestyle and workstyle so unique and distinctive that coworkers want to know why? If not, I challenge you to make whatever changes are necessary. So much depends on it: your own self-respect, the moral legacy that you leave for your family, the moral climate that you create where you work, your walk with God, even the advance of the gospel. For reasons like these I say that your integrity is your most valuable possession. Don't trade yours for a few measly candy bars of compromise. It's not worth it!

Sure, holding on to your integrity may cost you money, status, career advancement, or opportunity. It has even cost some Christians around the world their lives! Integrity costs, but lack of integrity will cost even more. Still, too many people seem willing to pay that awful price. Are you? Is there a price for which you *would* compromise your character? In the next chapter, we'll look at the tragic process many people go through as they make such a foolish bargain. By considering the dynamics of compromise, you can be warned against trading away your integrity.

CHAPTER FOUR

Why Good People Do Bad Things

*A young man from Proverbs 7 shows us
the steps to moral compromise.*

What is your reaction when you open your morning paper, only to learn that some prominent person has been discovered in a scandal? By now, given the sad history of fallen heroes that marks this past decade, you may feel jaundiced and cynical. *So what else is new?* may be your thought. But if a tragedy hits close to home—if someone you know or someone who means a lot to you is tarnished— you likely ask, "How could this happen? How could some- one who had so much going for him—who seemed so reliable, decent, respectable—allow himself to get mixed up in something like this?"

If you wonder that, you're not alone. Those who have fallen invariably wonder the same thing. From time to time I've been called in on situations where people in business or government have been undone by moral and ethical failures. They almost always ask me the very questions that I'd like to ask them: "How could this have happened? Where did I go wrong? Why did I have to end up like this?"

Those are such important questions that I want to devote this chapter to answering them. You see, most of us ask those questions, which are the right questions, at the wrong time! The time to ask is not after we've blown it, after we've compromised ourselves and brought disgrace and ruin on ourselves and others. The time to ask is *before* we're ever faced with temptation.

This was the thinking of Solomon, the author of most of the book of Proverbs. You may know that Proverbs is a series of instructions about life given by a father as he prepares his son to become a responsible adult. He's telling his son ahead of time what to expect, what to value, and what to avoid. His wisdom is preventive medicine from which we can learn a great deal that can help us avoid falling into compromise.

A MORALITY PLAY

In Proverbs 7, the father explains the dynamics of compromise. He wants his son to understand the process a person goes through in giving in to temptation. To illustrate his point, he describes a young man who gives in to the enticements of a prostitute. However, the lessons to be gained from this passage go far beyond the topic of sexual immorality. The instruction is a paradigm for dealing with temptations of all kinds. The dynamics of compromise are the same, no matter what form temptation takes. I'll cover seven principles from this passage in a moment.

First, notice how the father begins with a positive exhortation before he goes into his negative illustration (7:1-5):

My son, keep my words,
And treasure my commandments within you.
Keep my commandments and live,
And my teaching as the apple of your eye.

Bind them on your fingers;
Write them on the tablet of your heart.
Say to wisdom, "You are my sister,"
And call understanding your intimate friend;
That they may keep you from an adulteress,
From the foreigner who flatters with her words.

The father strongly urges his boy to hold on to wisdom. Treasure it, he says, keep it in front of you, in your conscious thoughts; use physical reminders to avoid forgetting it; memorize it; cherish it as you would your own family; make it your closest friend. And wisdom—the skill of applying God's Word to daily situations—is no less valuable, in as much as it is the means toward maintaining our integrity.

I'm struck with the strategies mentioned in the passage to help the son remember godly values. In our own culture, I could imagine any number of items to remind us of God's holy standards: a card on our desk or in our car with a Bible verse on it; a booklet in one's pocket or purse that urges faithfulness; a Post-it note on the bathroom mirror or inside our checkbook; maybe even a reminder jotted somewhere in our computer to encourage us toward godliness. I'm not suggesting gimmicks here. Instead, like the father in Proverbs 7, I'm eager that we take pains to consciously recall godly values and a commitment to Christlikeness as we go through a hectic day.

We need to cultivate an insatiable thirst for wisdom. Every day we need to drink deeply from God's Word, refreshing ourselves from His promises and replenishing our spiritual strength from His truth. This pursuit of wisdom must become a life-long passion. It's our number one protection against compromise.

The father in Proverbs 7 wants his son to turn out right. What loving parent wouldn't? Likewise, God wants the best for you and me. He longs that we enjoy moral purity and not be taken in by evil. The sad reality is that it's all too easy to compromise. Let's see how that happens as we consider seven principles in the psychology of compromise.

Compromise Flourishes When the Decision to Do Right Is Not Made Ahead of Time.

The father sets up the story by recounting something he has seen (Proverbs 7:6-7):

> For at the window of my house
> I looked out through my lattice,
> And I saw among the naive,
> I discerned among the youths,
> A young man lacking sense.

The illustration centers on a young man. Right away we can tell that he is headed for trouble, because he is described as "naive," a youth, and "lacking sense." If you know much about Proverbs, you know that this is not just a reference to his physical youth, but to his *moral immaturity.*

The fellow is "naive"; literally, he is "simple." In Proverbs, that means that he has no clear moral standards to guide his conduct. He's never made up his mind about the values he'll live by. He just lets himself behave however the prevailing conditions demand. When the guys want to act decent and kind, he becomes decent and kind. When they decide to tell dirty jokes and make fun of people and sneak to the porno theater, he's right there with them.

In short, this young man is a situational ethicist. He's not committed to evil, like the wicked person is, but he's not committed to good, either, like the wise person is. Morally speaking, he's on the fence. He can go either way, depending on the situation. That's moral immaturity.

I find a parallel between avoiding moral compromise and dieting. From time to time, when I need to lose a few pounds, I go on a diet. Having done this a number of times, I've learned that one of the secrets to successful dieting is to decide ahead of time—*before* I get to the table—what I will and will not eat. I have to make up my mind ahead of time to limit myself to one moderate helping, to avoid gravy and butter, and to say "no thank you" to dessert. If I don't, I'll never be able to resist once I'm served tempting dishes!

Overcoming moral temptations is just the same. You have to make up your mind ahead of time what you will and will not do. For instance, before you enter your workplace, make these decisions: you won't lie, no matter what; you won't pilfer supplies or cheat on your hours; you'll refrain from gossip and character assassination of coworkers; you'll never break the law; you won't engage in sexual immorality.

There are dozens of other decisions like these, which you can and should make ahead of time, that will keep you from compromise when the pressure is on. For instance, you could commit to the principles outlined in the next six chapters—H-O-N-E-S-T. But if you wait until temptation is staring you in the face, you'll likely give way.

Compromise Occurs When
You Underestimate Evil and Flirt with Temptation.

Proverbs 7:8-9 goes on to describe the young man's actions:

> Passing through the street near her corner;
> And he takes the way to her house,
> In the twilight, in the evening,
> In the middle of the night and in the darkness.

This fellow is playing with fire, and the prostitute hasn't even entered the story yet! But we know that something is coming because he is observed to be in the wrong place at the wrong time. He has no business in that part of town at that time of night (or day). It's obvious that he's looking for trouble, though a person in that type of situation would probably deny it if confronted.

This is the strange thing about compromise: It's something one doesn't want and yet wants very much. It begins with thinking about doing what is wrong, then imagining what it would be like, and then physically placing oneself in the conditions where compromise is possible. It occurs when we flirt with temptation—as this young man is doing.

It is fair to ask: When this fellow finally falls, will he be a passive victim who got ensnared by a woman, or did he choose to allow himself to be snared? I think verses 8-9 make it plain that he *chose* a path to moral defeat by flirting with danger.

Sometimes I run into someone who looks down on the idea that playing with evil inevitably leads to sin. He boasts about his ability to withstand, even though he places himself directly in temptation's path. To me, this is not only foolish, it is ungodly. For the person pursuing godliness makes every effort to keep himself just as pure as he can—not to get away with as much as he can.

Another statement I occasionally hear goes something like this: "I know all about living for God at work. I just follow the Golden Rule [or the Ten Commandments, or the Four-Way Test]. If I just follow that, everything else will take care of itself." Once a fellow even objected to my suggestion that he plan ahead of time to maintain his integrity. "It's unnecessary," he claimed. "If you start your day by praying, 'Lord, help me to do my best today,' everything will work out just fine."

I think this fellow and others who rely on simplistic formulas grossly underestimate evil in the workplace and the effort it takes to keep our ethical edge sharp. Perhaps they work in rather serene, neutral surroundings. But most of us face incredible situations at work that test our mettle and challenge our character. People lie. They cheat. They steal. They play political games. They sabotage our plans. They bicker and gossip. They evade responsibility. Sometimes we feel like we're in a jungle, where survival demands the ethics of expediency.

It's always dangerous to underestimate evil, because inevitably we'll meet a match who is stronger and craftier than we are—just as this youth does. This brings us to a third principle.

Compromise Is Always Just a Choice Away.
Another way to say that compromise is always a choice away is that compromise lurks everywhere. That's what Proverbs 7:10-11 tells us:

> And behold, a woman comes to meet him,
> Dressed as a harlot and cunning of heart.
> She is boisterous and rebellious;
> Her feet do not remain at home.

In this situation compromise lurks in the form of a prostitute. In that culture, a prostitute often would have been a married woman who would wait until her husband left and then entice other men into her bed—as she does with this young man.

Opportunities for compromise are everywhere. After all, sin is aggressive, always waiting for you, ready to pounce (see Genesis 4:7). Sexual immorality is one form of temptation, but there are numerous others: "Now in the streets, now in the squares, [lurking] by every corner" (verse 12). It's so important that we realize there is evil all around us and in us, and if we play with it, it will inevitably bring us down.

Three sources of evil may entice you to compromise. Recognizing them is a first step away from danger. Never underestimate their power! The first category is the evil that the Bible describes as "the world." The world is the value system of the people around you who do not put Christ first in their lives or thinking. He is given no part. First John 2:15-16 describes this system and warns us against it:

> Do not love the world, nor the things in the world. If any one loves the world, the love of the Father is not in him. For all that is in the world, the lust of the flesh and the lust of the eyes and the boastful pride of life, is not from the Father, but is from the world.

Every day in the workplace we rub up against the world. Certainly, the values and attitudes by which the business world operates in our culture tend to leave God out. In some cases it is completely opposed to Him. For example, many feel that success is measured only in dollars and cents. Likewise, they say significance comes from acquiring prestige and power. As for ethics and morality, they think that whatever is right for you is right. Ideas like these are opposed to biblical truth. They ignore what God has to say in these matters.

So as you enter the workplace, be aware—if you aren't already—that you'll inevitably face many opportunities to compromise. Don't flirt with it! Compromise is only a choice away!

Not only is there evil around us in the world, there is also evil present in ourselves. The Bible describes this internal tendency toward evil as "the flesh." Galatians 5:19-21 tells us what the flesh is capable of:

> Now the deeds of the flesh are evident, which are:
> immorality, impurity, sensuality, idolatry, sorcery,
> enmities, strife, jealousy, outbursts of anger, disputes,
> dissensions, factions, envying, drunkenness, carous-
> ing, and things like these, of which I forewarned you
> that those who practice such things shall not inherit
> the kingdom of God.

Do we really do things that are that bad? Yes! The Bible says we do. Some people already know they are capable of such evil; they have no trouble identifying their particular sins on the list mentioned. Others, of course, find it more difficult to name their fleshly ills, which is perhaps why Paul included the catchall phrase, "and things like these." Such things as a desire for revenge, a desire for more, and a desire for illicit sex would be examples.

The point is that not only are these many solicitations to compromise confronting us in the external environment, there are also many motivations from within to depart from godliness.

The third source of evil to be aware of is "the devil." Satan is real, and he is our sworn enemy. He has the ability to work in concert with the world and the flesh to entice us to compromise.

First Peter 5:8 tells us to watch out for Satan's wiles: "Be of sober spirit, be on the alert. Your adversary, the devil, prowls about like a roaring lion, seeking someone to devour." Note that Peter doesn't liken the devil to a barking poodle that harasses us but is fundamentally harmless. No, he's like a roaring lion! He's loose, he's dangerous, and he's hungry! Elsewhere in Scripture we find that he whispers rationalizations in our ear, he fuels our anger toward others, and he incites envy in us for the things that others have. The image is of a being who is more powerful than we are and whose purpose is to destroy us. He wants to trick us into disobedience. (Ephesians 6:10-18 tells us how to deal with Satan.)

The world, the flesh, and the devil—three sources of evil, enticing us to compromise. Like the prostitute in Proverbs 7, their temptations are everywhere. We need to be aware of that and have a healthy respect for the fact that compromise is always at hand, always just a choice away. It can happen to you, to me, to anyone—anytime, anywhere.

Compromise Entices Through Flattery and Fantasy. Having never made up his mind about his moral convictions, having placed himself directly in temptation's path, and having met someone who is far craftier than he, the youth in Proverbs 7 is ready to swallow all kinds of bait that will hook him into evil (verses 13-17):

> So she seizes him and kisses him,
> And with a brazen face she says to him:
> "I was due to offer peace offerings;
> Today I have paid my vows.
> Therefore I have come out to meet you,
> To seek your presence earnestly, and I have
>   found you.
> I have spread my couch with coverings,
> With colored linens of Egypt.
> I have sprinkled my bed
> With myrrh, aloes and cinnamon."

Notice the devices this woman uses to ensnare her victim. She opens with *flattery* (verses 13-15). Nearly all temptation has a bit of flattery in it, even if it's nothing more than the flattery of thinking you can "get away" with something.

Say, for instance, that you're an auto mechanic. An

elderly woman who knows little about cars brings hers in and asks you to fix it. She doesn't even know what the problem is. We'll say that the car has a corroded battery cable. You could fix it for under twenty dollars. Then comes temptation, and with it a bit of flattery. It occurs to you that you could sell this woman a new battery and make more money. There's a bit of flattery in just being able to imagine that you're in control, you're the one with options. That's a rather appealing position to be in, whether you take advantage of it or not.

In addition to flattery, the woman in Proverbs 7 also uses *fantasy* (verses 16-17). She paints a picture of pleasure and delight: "Wouldn't it be wonderful if. . . ?" Temptation is so often a battle for the imagination.

Let's return to the example of the mechanic. If you sell the lady a battery, you could pocket as much as fifty dollars. It's easy for you to dream of what you could do with that money: buy a new fishing reel, tool, or item of clothing, go out for a nice dinner, pay off a debt. Likewise, all temptation paints a picture for our imagination, showing us how much "better off" we'd be if only we'd compromise.

Compromise Ensnares
Through Rationalization and Deception.

> "Come, let us drink our fill of love until morning;
> Let us delight ourselves with caresses.
> For the man is not at home,
> He has gone on a long journey;
> He has taken a bag of money with him,
> At full moon he will come home."
> With her many persuasions she entices him;
> With her flattering lips she seduces him.
> (verses 18-21)

The next lure in the adulteress's tackle box is *rationalization* (Proverbs 7:18), and that's a sure winner. A rationalization simply applies a good purpose to something that is inherently wrong. She calls what they are about to do drinking their fill of love. But it's not love, it's wrong, immoral, and offensive to God. We all are geniuses at coming up with good reasons for bad actions. The harlot attempts to give the action legitimacy, taking him one step closer to disaster.

I'm amazed at some of the rationalizations I read and hear about. You're no doubt familiar with many of them:

- "Everybody does that."
- "It's a small compromise—just bending the rules."
- "The company knows that everyone 'pads' their expense accounts, so go ahead, they're expecting it."
- "They owe me one!"
- "It'll all come out in the wash."
- "It's the way the system operates."
- "If I don't do it, I'll lose respect."
- "Who's going to know?"
- "Once I get to the top [by cheating and deception] I'll fix the system."

My personal favorite is an explanation made by a man who cheated a customer on a sales deal: "It's okay, I'm planning to give a lot of my profits to my church." I think God would tell him, "Keep it, pal!"

Next, the woman assures the victim that there will be no consequences to the crime. Her husband "has gone on a long journey; he has taken a bag of money with him, at full moon he will come home" (verses 19-20). Her point is that he will be gone and no one will know about their action.

Evil tries to convince us that no one will know and there will be no consequences. We don't ever speed in front of a policeman. We do it when we "think" there will be no consequences. But of course, there are always consequences.

There have been cases of business executives who knowingly misrepresented their product to the consumer. In their hearts they must have been tricked into believing that they could get by with it. But often after felony convictions, this idea is dispelled.

In this life there are jails and lawsuits, and people are fired or fined. Reputations are destroyed, businesses collapse. We will reap what we sow. Even if our wrongdoing escapes the notice of our fellowmen, it never escapes the notice of our Creator. We all go on to our own reward—whatever that may be. We'll return to this thought in a moment. But first, consider the next principle.

Compromise Finally Occurs with a Refusal to Think About the Rightness of Our Actions.

The adulteress has used all her wiles to get this simpleton into bed with her. He's an easy mark. We almost feel like he's a helpless victim, like a lamb being led to the slaughter.

Proverbs 7:22 describes it: "Suddenly he follows her, as an ox goes to the slaughter." This is an interesting way to describe the moment of compromise. After all the woman has said to him, he is like a dumb, helpless ox about to be slaughtered. And yet, it's his choice. "Suddenly" he makes up his mind, and "he follows her." He *chooses* to follow her—into ruin.

Compromise is always our decision. And usually it's a sudden decision: We don't want to pray; we don't want to reflect on Scripture; we don't want to consult our conscience; we just do what we want to do—suddenly!

In the '60s people used to joke by using Flip Wilson's famous line: "The devil made me do it!" Watergate and more recently "Irangate" have made it fashionable to plead a different excuse: "I was only following orders!" But we can't evade accountability before God so easily. If we fall into sin, it's because we *choose* to sin. No one *makes* us sin. As James 1:14-15 explains:

> But each one is tempted when he is carried away and enticed by his own lust. Then when lust has conceived, it gives birth to sin; and when sin is accomplished, it brings forth death.

Compromise Always Costs.
No matter how secret or private our actions, no matter how well we cover our tracks, a moral compromise will always cost us greatly. Proverbs 7:22-23 says,

> Suddenly he follows her,
> As an ox goes to the slaughter,
> Or as one in fetters to the discipline of a fool,
> Until an arrow pierces through his liver;
> As a bird hastens to the snare,
> So he does not know that it will cost him his life.

It's not exactly clear what happens to this fellow. Perhaps the husband returns home suddenly, flies into a jealous rage, and kills him on the spot. Maybe his sin is discovered by the community, and he is executed in accordance with Mosaic Law (Leviticus 20:10). Or it could be that he contracts a venereal disease and slowly wastes away. Perhaps no one ever discovers his sin, yet God strikes him down. Whatever the specifics, his sin has definite consequences: "It will cost him his life."

All sin has consequences. Those consequences may come in this life or in the next, but we can never escape the repercussions of moral compromise. In the last chapter I mentioned several possibilities: a tremendous loss of self-respect, a tarnished legacy for our families, a missed moral impact on others, a darkness or obstacle in our fellowship with God, and a breakdown in the advance of the gospel. Many more could be mentioned. And I could illustrate each with tragic, true stories about people who, like the naive young fool in Proverbs 7, traded their most valuable possession—their integrity—for a few brief moments of pleasure, a few dollars, or a few ego-biscuits.

How did moral compromise happen? Through (1) a failure to commit ahead of time to doing the right thing; (2) underestimating evil and flirting with dangerous temptations, thus being exposed to far more powerful evils; (3) a failure to recognize the numerous forms of compromise lurking at every corner of life; (4) a failure to recognize the smooth flatteries and enticing fantasies of temptation; (5) succumbing to slick rationalizations; (6) a sudden, deliberate choice to give in to sin; and (7) a failure to consider the costly consequences of sin.

The remarkable thing about every person I've known who has compromised morally or ethically is that he is just like you and me: no better or worse, no stronger or weaker. That means that you and I are at least as vulnerable. The most dangerous attitude we could ever adopt is one that many of the fallen adopted: "It can't happen to me!" Oh, yes it can! First Corinthians 10:12 warns us: "Therefore let him who thinks he stands take heed lest he fall."

Not long ago, I saw a series of photos in a pictorial magazine about José Cubera. Apparently, Cubera was one of the top bullfighters in Spain. The photos showed how he had lanced a bull with the last and most deadly thrust of his swords, and the bull had fallen in the dust of the arena. As the spectators jumped to their feet with a roar, Cubera raised his arms to accept their thundering acclamation.

The photos showed that Cubera had turned his back on the felled animal. It suddenly rallied and, in a final desperate rage, gored the proud bullfighter right through the back! Both man and beast expired in a pool of blood.

"Let him who thinks he stands *take heed* lest he fall." It can happen to anyone! Therefore, we all must stay on our guard to decide ahead of time to do the right thing, lest moral compromise attack us when we least expect it, and we fall victim to it. In the next six chapters, we'll consider specific areas in which you can take steps to maintain ethical purity.

CHAPTER FIVE

H—Honesty

*Being honest to God means
you don't cheat or steal.*

What's the difference between having integrity and hav- ing a good reputation? Aren't they really the same thing? Perhaps. Certainly they're related, and it's hard to have one without the other. But there is one important difference: A reputation is what you do when everyone is looking; integrity is what you do when no one is looking.

How about you? When no one else is around or no one else could possibly find out, what do you do? Are you like the young simpleton in Proverbs 7, who traded his integrity— and his life—for a wasted night with a worthless woman? Or are you like the fine china I mentioned in chapter 3, set apart for God's special purposes and genuinely pure out of love for Him?

You will recall from our discussion of Proverbs 7 that one of the keys to keeping your ethical edge sharp is decid- ing ahead of time what you will do in the midst of tempta- tion. Each of the next six chapters will present a biblical principle of integrity. Let me encourage you to make a firm and definite commitment ahead of time to each one. Please know that there is much more to integrity than one book could cover. But if you can achieve a measure of success with these principles you will be ethically distinctive!

Remember, no matter how much integrity you have, you can never completely master biblical integrity. In fact it is important to recognize that there are different levels of integrity.

The most common level of integrity is what I call "out of trouble" honesty. At this level people are motivated to be honest by fear of reprisal. If they avoid reprisal, they are proud of themselves. On the other hand, they feel that it is okay to get away with whatever they can.

Other people have a kind of "selective honesty." At this level of integrity they decide which areas of integrity they will obey and hope their obedience to these few areas will overcome disobedience to the rest. Commonly, they compare themselves to others on the basis of their strengths, but are not interested in learning about their own weaknesses or in making a change.

The third level of integrity I only see in limited numbers. The people at this level are passionate in their desire to honor Christ—doing His work, His way. They have "progressive integrity." They realize that biblical integrity is not natural; it takes focused attention. They have learned that the scope of biblical integrity is broader than a few principles easily mastered. They know that the human heart is capable of rationalizing almost anything and have cultivated a healthy mistrust of themselves, allowing their actions to come under regular scrutiny of God's Word. They come to the Scriptures with great humility, knowing that each pass at a scriptural principle could bring new application and insight. Finally, they realize that God is gracious enough to us to not reveal all the sin in our life at once, choosing to progressively reveal areas in our life that He wants to conquer. Thus, honesty is a path we are on, not a point we achieve.

I want to approach the next six chapters with the perspective of pursuing "progressive honesty." We will consider six principles, using the acrostic "H-O-N-E-S-T-Y." H stands for being honest by not cheating or stealing; O, for obeying authority; N, for no deception; E, for encouraging conflict resolution; S, for sexual fidelity; and T, for trustworthiness. In this chapter we will focus on the first of these principles.

AN HONEST PERSON DOES NOT CHEAT OR STEAL

Does this topic even need discussion? Isn't it obvious that a follower of Christ should not cheat or steal? Well, please remember that there are levels of honesty even in the realm of cheating and stealing. Let's look at some common examples:

- "Time theft" from coming into work late, excessive breaks or lunches.
- Energy theft on the emotional level, allowing personal problems or non-work interests to distract you when you should be giving your full attention to the job.
- Cheating on expense reports, e.g. taking a friend to lunch and calling it "business," claiming personal purchases as business expenses.
- Cheating on income tax deductions through neglecting to report cash income or claiming deductions that are not totally valid.
- Use of the company long distance line for personal calls.
- Pilfering supplies such as food from a restaurant, pens and paper, or using the copier at work for

personal copies without paying for it.

• Not correcting an overpayment from the insurance company, or from anyone else.

• Choosing to do work that is not necessary such as unneeded surgery, unneeded work on an automobile.

• Accepting payment for work not done, or delivery of supplies not ordered or paid for.

• Accepting a "gift" that improperly directs you to lower your standards. For example, a purchasing agent taking a gift from a salesman, and then buying his inferior product.

• Improperly taking a client from a competitor.

• Violating copyright laws through illegal copying of computer software, books, music, videos.

How about in your career field? What are some of the common forms of cheating or stealing you see? As I travel I am absolutely amazed to hear of the creative ways to cheat in various jobs!

In a few moments we'll study how God views all this. First, let's define some terms. Cheating and stealing are twins. Cheating is getting an unfair advantage; stealing is getting something that does not rightfully belong to you or keeping someone else from getting what is rightfully theirs. Both are common. Both are wrong.

A biblical study finds no confusion about how the Lord views either of these issues.

"You shall not steal." (Exodus 20:15)

"You shall not steal, nor deal falsely, nor lie to one another. . . . You shall not oppress your neighbor, nor rob him. The wages of a hired man are not to remain with you all night until morning." (Leviticus 19:11,13)

The mood of these verses is authoritative. It is the mood of a father offering his sternest warning to his children about something that could harm them. The prohibition is short, direct, and forceful. Notice, too, the issue of withholding what is due is said in the same breath as stealing.

In the book of Proverbs we see how gravely God views this activity of dishonesty relative to other sins: "Differing weights and differing measures, both of them are abominable to the LORD" (Proverbs 20:10).

The context of this verse was an ancient agrarian culture. A farmer would bring his grain to a dealer who would weigh it and pay the farmer an appropriate amount, then sell it in the market. Rocks were used as the countermeasure on the scales to determine weight. If the dealer used a twelve-pound rock and said it weighed ten pounds when measuring a load from the farmer, he would get twelve pounds of grain for the price of ten. If the dealer then selected an eight-pound rock when a consumer wanted to buy a ten-pound load, he would receive payment on ten pounds for only eight pounds of grain. Thus, cheating the farmer and the customer. This is using differing weights and measures.

In the book of Proverbs only a few sins are considered "abominable" what the Lord "hates," including cheating and stealing. Here are some others: murder, lying, and wickedness (Proverbs 6:16) and evil plans (15:26). This implies that God has terribly strong feelings about cheating and stealing in any form! But it is also clear that any advantage gained by cheating is illusory:

Ill-gotten gains do not profit. (Proverbs 10:2)

Bread obtained by falsehood is sweet to a man,
But afterward his mouth will be filled with gravel.
(Proverbs 20:17)

Apparently, the God who created the world we live in has set certain rules of life and this is one of them. Cheating or stealing bring only short-term pleasure.

Perhaps it's easy to see this in our day with recent allegations in the business community. For instance, the Chrysler Corporation recently was discovered to have rolled back the odometers of the executive cars to make the cars look new. A black mark on their reputation.

The truth of Proverbs 20:17 also applies to the "lesser sins" in the list of common examples at the beginning of this chapter. It seems like everywhere I go, I find at least one person in the crowd who will object to this line of reasoning, saying something like this: "Okay so stealing is wrong, we know that. But if I started to scrutinize every little action at the coffee machine, or copier, or on my expense account, I'd never have time for anything else. Why don't you take this message to Wall Street where the real crooks are?"

First, I feel honored any time I go to Wall Street. Second, the question betrays some unfortunate thinking.

God does care about our honesty at every level. In fact honesty and dishonesty are both habit forming. What we do in the small issues of life sets the stage for bigger issues. What we do at the copier, on the phone, in front of the mail machine are important and set the stage for how we will respond to greater temptations that *will come!*

It is also true that once we violate our conscience in an area it is easier to do it the next time. Before long, our heart becomes callous.

Not long ago I received a letter from a man in prison who had heard me on a radio program. He and three other men had been involved in a defense contracting company. The president of the firm won the Entrepreneur of the Year Award presented to him by then President Reagan.

The letter writer had accepted Christ as a young boy. He

told me that in his early twenties he started compromising his integrity in "little" things. They became easier and easier. Within a few years his company showed rocket growth and apparent success. But—as his letter revealed—the growth was fueled by a government scam that extracted thousands of dollars of taxpayers' money. The same week I received his letter I had lunch at the Justice Department with a prosecutor. When I told him about the letter, his face turned white. He was the one who had convicted the man. He was astounded that the prisoner knew Christ. Compromise is habit forming. "Except for the grace of God go I."

YOUR WORLD

At this point, I want you to think of the unique forms of stealing and cheating in your occupation. The clearer you are on what they are, the easier it will be for you to avoid them.

If in reading this material and reflecting on it, a particular action comes to mind where you have blown it, take the appropriate steps now to set things right. First, admit to God what you have done wrong. Acknowledge that it was wrong. Second, accept His complete forgiveness and do not dwell on your sense of guilt. To not accept forgiveness for a wrong done is to insult the Lord who forgives you. (More will be said on this in chapter 14.) Third, make restitution. If you cheated on an expense report, give the money back. If you cheated on your income tax, it's easy enough to fix. You see, how you handle yourself when you've blown it is as much a part of your integrity as not doing wrong in the first place. It might be embarrassing to admit wrong to your boss or a coworker, but clearing your name is much more important. Sometimes you have to choose whether you are going to be a fool before men or before God.

As we conclude this short discussion of honesty, let's remember the lessons of Proverbs 7. Decide ahead of time that you will not cheat or steal—no matter how much money, status, or fame you might receive. Make honesty your habit. Guard yourself from rationalization. Never underestimate evil or your own capacity to rationalize it. Bring your work day under constant scriptural scrutiny. Depend on God for victory over evil, especially through prayer. Assume that what you do is in full view of the God who loves you deeply. Remember that the consequences of cheating or stealing are real and disastrous. But if you do fall, quickly take the proper steps to reconcile with God and make restitution with your fellowman. Proverbs 11:2 says, "A false balance is an abomination to the LORD, *but a just weight is His delight*" (emphasis added).

Keeping your ethical edge sharp makes you a delight to the Lord. God made you for a purpose. As you go to work each day you should feel the sunshine of His approval. Neither you nor I will be perfect until we get to Heaven. But we can have "progressive integrity."

In the next chapter we will shift to another aspect of your "edge"—how you deal with authority.

CHAPTER SIX

O—Obey Authority

*How you relate to your boss speaks volumes
about your character.*

In June of 1968, I headed off to college at the United States Air Force Academy. You may know that the first twelve weeks of the school are a nightmare for freshman. We were made to feel lower than slime! We ran up and down mountains, stood at attention for what seemed like years, and memorized more facts about aircraft than we ever dreamed existed. But the hardest part of the training program was mealtime. Part of the discipline was learning to eat with only three chews per bite. (Try it sometime.) Another part was sitting at the table with food under your nose for several meals in a row without eating.

Toward the end of the program, my birthday came. Miraculously, my group of six classmates (called an *Element*) was permitted to have cake and Coke in my room. It was like heaven on earth! Keep in mind that we had missed many meals during the twelve weeks and had each lost ten to twenty pounds.

While the group hovered over the cake and ice cream, upperclassmen circled in the hallways waiting for some minor infraction by one of us so they could stop the fun and get us back to feeling like the slime they knew we were. After guzzling a Coke I began to feel pretty good. I had a piece of cake and felt even better. So I did it. I walked out of the room—to the shock and horror of my classmates—and up to the sternest upperclassman in my squadron. Following protocol, I went up to him and said, "Sir, may I make a statement?"

He stuck his nose an inch from mine and yelled, "What do you want, squat?" (*Squat* is a degrading word for a freshman.)

When my moment came, I belched in his face. After that things went down hill. He got several of his classmates together, and we spent the better part of the evening discussing the issue of authority. What I mean is we spent the whole evening, there was nothing *better* about it. That night I learned that it is best to both follow and honor authority!

ALL LEGITIMATE AUTHORITY IS FROM GOD

The place to begin any discussion about authority is to affirm that all authority is an expression of God's authority. This does not mean, of course, that every authority is wielded with godliness. Obviously, there are many governments, officials, employers, and other power brokers who use their authority in very inhuman and evil ways. Nevertheless, God Himself, as the *ultimate* authority, has determined that people should not operate in chaos and anarchy, but that some type of authority will maintain control.

The forms that such control takes vary widely from culture to culture. Some are relatively primitive and informal; others are highly structured and authoritarian. Whatever sort of system God's people may happen to live and work under, God commands us (1 Peter 2:13-17),

> Submit yourselves for the Lord's sake to every human institution, whether to a king as the one in authority, or to governors as sent by him for the punishment of evildoers and the praise of those who do right. For such is the will of God that by doing right you may silence the ignorance of foolish men. Act as free men, and do not use your freedom as a covering for evil, but use it as bondslaves of God. Honor all men; love the brotherhood, fear God, honor the king.

As God's people, we are to submit to the human authorities over us, whether they are the government, our employer, our stockholders, or whomever. Yielding to such authorities is an expression of yielding to God's authority. But how submission is expressed in various work environments may be a little different.

For instance, an acquaintance of mine builds houses. His company has a very loose hierarchy in which he makes most of the major decisions affecting company expenditures and policies, while his supervisors handle on-site details. Given the nature of the work, everyone more or less knows what to do. While construction is a business where supervisors generally ride hard on their crews, it's still not very authoritarian.

How different that is from a close friend of mine who used to work in a high-level job at the Veterans Administration. With 240,000 employees staffing 172 hospitals, fifty-eight regional offices, more than 100 nursing homes, and several domiciliaries, in each of the fifty states plus the Philippines, Europe, and Puerto Rico, the VA is a completely different institution. The authority infrastructure is vastly more complex. Working there in submission to that authority looks much different than it does on a work crew in the suburbs.

In both cases, God desires that the workers submit to authority, even though that means something different to a VA worker than to a carpenter. But you as the worker have to determine who you answer to, how much latitude you have in making your own choices, and what submission requires in your circumstances.

All across the work world, we're finding that workers are assuming more authority and control over their work. In an information society we find more "knowledge workers" who work, not with their hands, but with ideas, concepts, and theories. In many cases, these workers know far more than their employers. Consider the implications of that for the politics of the workplace!

"Submit yourselves for the Lord's sake to every human institution," Peter says. The principle here is that everyone is accountable to someone, and every one of us is accountable to God. Whether or not our superiors are as direct and obvious as a drill sergeant, our biblical responsibility is to submit. Let's consider how we can do that in two major categories of authority: the government and our employer.

SUBMISSION TO THE GOVERNMENT

The Bible is very clear about our responsibility to obey governmental authority. We saw this teaching in the 1 Peter passage earlier. Of course, the classic text in this regard is Romans 13:1-7:

> Let every person be in subjection to the governing authorities. For there is no authority except from God, and those which exist are established by God. Therefore he who resists authority has opposed the ordinance of God; and they who have opposed will receive condemnation upon themselves. For rulers

are not a cause of fear for good behavior, but for evil. Do you want to have no fear of authority? Do what is good, and you will have praise from the same; for it is a minister of God to you for good. But if you do what is evil, be afraid; for it does not bear the sword for nothing; for it is a minister of God, an avenger who brings wrath upon the one who practices evil. Wherefore it is necessary to be in subjection, not only because of wrath, but also for conscience' sake.

For because of this you also pay taxes, for rulers are servants of God, devoting themselves to this very thing. Render to all what is due them: tax to whom tax is due; custom to whom custom; fear to whom fear; honor to whom honor.

Notice again the principle that government is established by God. In fact, "rulers are servants of God," Paul says. That may be hard to swallow given some of the shenanigans we see in government from time to time. Yet keep in mind that Paul was writing this to citizens of Rome, whose emperor at the time was *Nero*.

Today, when we think of the regulation by the government in our work, we think of taxes, laws, and standards that govern industry. Paul says quite plainly that we're to pay our taxes and submit to the laws. Having said that, however, we immediately run into questions as we seek to apply this principle in our society today. We enjoy a great deal more freedom and self-determination than Paul's readers could have possibly imagined. We have access to the courts and to lawmakers, where we can challenge what we regard as unfair laws and press for change. Furthermore, many regulations, particularly in the tax code, are not clear cut; they can apply differently to different situations.

The question, then, is how do we submit to governmental authority in our particular society? Let me suggest a few principles.

First, *we must always obey laws that are clear and unequivocal.* This is a decision we need to make ahead of time—that we will obey the law. For instance, in the trucking industry, there are certain standards regarding how much weight certain sizes of trucks can carry, what kinds of cargo are permissible in traveling though certain areas, and what level of training and experience are required for certain kinds of driving. If you're employed in the trucking industry, it's your responsibility as a believer to comply with such rules and regulations. They are clear and specific. Biblically, you need to obey them.

Recently, I was in Toronto speaking on the subject of biblical integrity. I went through the acrostic H-O-N-E-S-T-Y, which contains the idea of being subject to authority. Following the message a man approached me with a serious look in his eye almost as though he was angry. He said, "Doug, you just cost me $35,000." I asked him what he meant. Apparently, he was a commercial builder of condominiums. He had just bought a lot zoned for a triplex, but planned to build a fourplex on it because he thought the local officials wouldn't say anything. The extra unit would net him $35,000, but it was against the law! He knew what Christ wanted him to do. If it's the law, it's the law.

This brings us to a second principle: *By submitting to laws that are clear and unequivocal, we give ourselves an advantage in discerning how to handle laws that are unclear.* Perhaps it's only a psychological advantage, but by submitting to laws that are easily understood, we show that we have made up our minds to obey the law. That will prove enormously helpful when it comes time to tackle the gray areas. For instance, many stockbrokers and investment bankers are now struggling with the nuances of recent developments in insider trading laws. It's hard to be precise about what is and isn't permissible. However, a habit pattern of following authority will stand you in good stead for thinking through the thorny dilemmas. I'll say more on gray areas later.

Let me suggest a third principle: *In striving to maintain integrity when rules and regulations are unclear, it's important to seek professional as well as biblical wisdom.* In matters of tax law, for instance, I suggest that you seek advice from an accountant or a lawyer who has integrity. Such a person may or may not be a Christian. What matters most is that he is honest and willing to help you comply with the law, not someone who tries to circumvent it.

However, I also encourage you to discuss your situation with other believers, especially ones who have faced similar circumstances and who are committed to a lifestyle of integrity. There's a real benefit to getting advice and insight when dealing with complex situations where there doesn't seem to be any one right answer. Our tendency is to make decisions on the basis of only how it benefits us, not what is fundamentally the right thing to do. We need the objectivity of others.

Finally, in dealing with governmental standards, *we should not shrink from exercising our rights as American citizens to press for change and justice.* I say this because there's a tendency among Christians to equate submission with passivity. The Bible tells us to submit to the government. But in our system of government, we have the freedom and the right to challenge the law and those who make it and enforce it. Where we feel an injustice is being done, we should not shy away from speaking up. That may mean filing a grievance, lobbying a lawmaker for a certain vote, campaigning among our associates to support a certain viewpoint, or taking legal action against an unfair situation.

Our guiding principle should be to promote godliness, integrity, and justice.

By the way, these same principles for dealing with government regulations also apply to dealing with government officials. In many industries, the government's inspectors, lawyers, and regulators are regularly looking over the shoulders of workers. If this is the case for you, how do you treat such officials? Do you try to see how much you can get away with? Or do you seek to comply with the agreed-upon standards?

Obviously, these officials sometimes can be obtrusive and difficult to deal with. (I'm sure some of them feel similarly toward you!) But remember, they are "servants of God," according to Romans 13, to whom you owe respect and submission. They are also human beings to whom you owe love and compassion. And they are fellow-workers, who have the right to be treated with dignity and value for the work they do.

SUBMISSION TO YOUR EMPLOYER

The most direct expression of authority in your workplace obviously comes from your employer or boss. Did you know that how you respond to your boss is a direct reflection of your response to Christ's authority? Colossians 3:22-24 says,

> Slaves, in all things obey those who are your masters
> on earth, not with external service, as those who
> merely please men, but with sincerity of heart, fearing
> the Lord. Whatever you do, do your work heartily, as
> for the Lord rather than for men; knowing that from
> the Lord you will receive the reward of the inheri-
> tance. It is the Lord Christ whom you serve.

Paul addresses slaves, who were the dominant group of workers in that culture. Sometimes you may feel like a slave in your job. But those in Paul's audience were real slaves, conquered people who carried out the menial, labor-intensive tasks of that society. Yet the principles of submission that applied to them apply to you and me as well.

What's remarkable is that the way we relate to our boss and the authority structures at work is ultimately the way we relate to Christ's authority. He is our ultimate Boss. Ephesians 6:5-8 reinforces this principle:

> Slaves, be obedient to those who are your masters according to the flesh, with fear and trembling, in the sincerity of your heart, as to Christ; not by way of eye-service, as men-pleasers, but as slaves of Christ, doing the will of God from the heart. With good will render service, as to the Lord, and not to men, knowing that whatever good thing each one does, this he will receive back from the Lord, whether slave or free.

The clear teaching of these two passages is that we're to submit to our earthly employers. We're to follow their directions, carry out their assignments to the best of our ability, and genuinely follow their leadership. We're also to comply with company standards and policies. This isn't to say that we have to be a "company man" who never disagrees or rocks the boat. But it does mean that we're to seek to serve the objectives and goals of the business as if Christ Himself were running the company.

So, for instance, if you're a female flight attendant and you're pregnant, you have a biblical responsibility to honor a policy regarding how late into your pregnancy you can fly. Or suppose your employer has a dress code; you need to honor it. If you work for an hourly wage, or if your boss sets particular work hours, you need to show up on time, prepared to get the job done. If you have reports to fill out, you need to complete them accurately and on time. These are the kinds of practical ways in which you can demonstrate your submission to Christ through your submission to your employer. After all, both of these passages speak of a final performance review—not one administered by our boss, but one administered by the Boss, Jesus Christ. What will He say to you? How will you be rewarded for your work?

This has a direct bearing on the issue of excellence in your work. When I was in the Air Force, we would go through a routine at our air base when an inspection team from Washington was coming through. Everyone went into overdrive sprucing up the grounds, facilities, and equipment in preparation for the inspection. Then when it was over, everyone would go back to his old habits.

That's what Paul called working "by way of eyeservice, as men-pleasers"; doing well only when the boss has his eye on you. But integrity has to do with our behavior when no one is watching—no one, that is, except God. When we're out making sales calls, when we're alone in our office, when we're making deliveries, when we're at a convention—when we're all alone, do we still work as if the boss were right there next to us? We should, because our ultimate Boss is!

How we relate to authority has a direct bearing on our testimony for the cause of Christ. Consider Titus 2:9-10 (NIV):

> Teach slaves to be subject to their masters in everything, to try to please them, not to talk back to them, and not to steal from them, but to show that they can be fully trusted, so that in every way they will make the teaching about God our Savior attractive.

Notice the specific behaviors mentioned here: your compliance with your boss's authority, the excellence of your work, the way you resolve conflicts, the integrity with which you treat company property, the trustworthiness and reliability you demonstrate. These are the ways you "make the teaching about God our Savior attractive." In a real sense, how you treat your boss will color his and others' perceptions of what Christianity is all about. First Timothy 6:1 makes a similar point:

> Let all who are under the yoke as slaves regard their own masters as worthy of all honor so that the name of God and our doctrine may not be spoken against.

This passage makes it plain that a lack of submissiveness to your employer does far more than injure your own career prospects. It also injures God's reputation, for it gives unbelievers a reason to despise Christ and His teaching. By the way, if your boss is already a believer, you have even more reason to honor his authority. I hear incredible stories from Christian employers about Christian employees who try to take advantage of them because they are believers. Paul goes on to warn against this very problem (6:2):

> And let those who have believers as their masters not be disrespectful to them because they are brethren, but let them serve them all the more, because those who partake of the benefit are believers and beloved. Teach and preach these principles.

"This is all well and good," I hear someone saying. "But you don't know *my* boss! You can't imagine what I have to put up with in my company. I'm all for submission. But what do you do when your boss is really unfair or your company is totally immoral?" These are excellent questions because they remind us that submission to the authority of our employers is not a simple matter. Scripture does give us help here through several important principles.

First, *no matter how unfair or immoral your boss is, you still have a responsibility to honor and respect his authority, even if you can't respect him as a person.* First Peter 2:18-20 tells us,

> Servants, be submissive to your masters with all respect, not only to those who are good and gentle, but also to those who are unreasonable. For this finds favor, if for the sake of conscience toward God a man bears up under sorrows when suffering unjustly. For what credit is there if, when you sin and are harshly treated, you endure it with patience? But if when you do what is right and suffer for it you patiently endure it, this finds favor with God.

I frequently hear from people who are mistreated at work because of their commitment to Christ. Sometimes these injustices are more imagined than real, but sometimes it's a clear-cut case of persecution. I recall one man who had been at his job for many years. He had come to faith late in life and really wanted to honor God in his work.

One day the man's employer decided to promote a younger man to a supervisory position. This was a blow to the older man for several reasons. First, he was disappointed because he had hoped for the supervisor's job himself. Furthermore, the man who got the job had previously worked under him; the job change reversed their roles, so that he was now under his former subordinate. Most disturbing of all was the fact that the younger man despised Christianity, and now he was using his position to abuse the believer. Apparently his attacks were quite vicious and difficult to defend against, since they were tied to aspects of the work.

As we talked about what this older man should do, I turned to the 1 Peter 2 passage and reminded him of his responsibility to do all he could to submit to the authority over him—even an unreasonable, unjust one. He was encouraged by the fact that what mattered was not the favor (or disfavor) shown him by the supervisor, but the favor promised him from the Lord for doing the right thing in the midst of difficult conditions.

There are limits, however, in this matter of compliance. A second principle has to do with obeying God rather than your boss: *You must decide up front what you will and will not do regardless of what the authority over you asks.* In other words, you need to determine your convictions and commitments in matters of integrity. What will you hang on to, no matter what the cost?

For instance, you should decide up front that you will not lie. Period. That way, if your boss ever asks you to lie, you don't have to fret and sweat about whether or not you should or shouldn't. You can immediately say you won't do that. Likewise, you won't cheat or steal or deal dishonestly in any other way.

I realize that conflict will doubtless result from your refusal to carry out your boss's dirty work. But conflict like that is appropriate and far more preferable than the internal conflict you'll go through as a believer if you violate your integrity. Furthermore, as Christians we follow in a noble tradition of men and women who have given their very lives to stand for what is right. What is the displeasure of a boss, or even the loss of a job, by comparison?

In chapter 1, I mentioned my friend Charlie, who was the CEO of a major franchiser in the food service industry.

The parent company of his firm was negotiating the sale of the conglomerate to an investment group. As an important member of the management team, Charlie was called to Manhattan to help in the sale.

Upon his arrival, he learned that the prospective buyer was offering an extremely good price per share for the stock of his company. Nevertheless, he was asked to present numbers to the buyer that were even higher. In fact, the proposed numbers were so inflated that Charlie felt they amounted to a gross distortion of reality—a lie. It was as if someone were selling a car that was worth about $10,000, but a prospective buyer offers $14,000 for it, so the seller counters by asking for $20,000. Good business, maybe, but bad ethics.

At any rate, in conscience Charlie said no. He refused to inflate the price. He offered to present numbers that were in line with the price bid, which was at least realistic. But he would not represent something he didn't believe was true. As a result, he was fired on the spot.

He's never regretted his decision. He had decided ahead of time that his integrity was worth more than his job, and that his allegiance to Christ outweighed his allegiance to the company. That's the kind of bedrock commitment we need more of: people willing to pay any price to maintain their integrity.

Having said that, of course, I'm not suggesting that Christians walk off the job every time there's a dispute over matters of principle. Charlie stood up for his convictions, and it cost him his job, but that's not always how things work out. As you confront situations in your workplace, you need to consider three questions as you decide how to respond.

First, *is the issue major or minor?* Not every conflict is worth resigning over; some are. If you're asked by your boss to defraud a customer, lie to the government, or accept a bribe, you should probably respond by stating that you don't operate like that, and if you have to do so to work there, then you'll find other work. After all, if you have to do wrong to be on the team, you're on the wrong team.

But not every issue is such a big deal. Pick your battles carefully, and don't become a moral policeman trying to right every wrong in the system. Charlie took a major stand, but he'd tell you that this was not his way of dealing with all the things he saw in the corporate world in the twenty-five years prior to that moment.

This brings us to the second question: *When should you act?* In our book *Your Work Matters to God* (NavPress, 1987), you will find an entire chapter devoted to evil in the workplace. We suggest that there are four types of circumstances that should trigger appropriate action on your part: (1) when you are called upon to do what is clearly wrong; (2) when your own conscience is violated; (3) when it is within your power to avoid evil; and (4) when innocent people stand to be affected.

A third question has to do with confrontation: *How should you approach an unjust or immoral boss?* At some point in your career, you *will* face such a situation. What should you do? I know some Christians will march into their boss's office and start quoting Scripture and raising heck. Personally, I believe that's the wrong thing to do, especially if the boss is an unbeliever.

You see, in general, people who have no relationship with the Lord will not be very responsive to Bible verses about right and wrong. Instead, they'll be antagonized. A better way to handle the confrontation is to lay out the facts as you understand them, and then argue on the basis of what is good and right, or on the basis of consequences or reputation. Argue on any basis that is meaningful to that individual. Then offer an alternative course of action that would be more in line with what you believe is right.

Of course, if the person is a believer, by all means bring in appropriate Scriptures and biblical principles. Yet even here, use the Bible not as a weapon to beat him down, but as a floodlight to provide insight and clarity in the midst of moral darkness and confusion. Galatians 6:1 urges us to treat other believers with gentleness, compassion, and humility as we challenge them on moral issues (see also Colossians 3:12-13):

> Brethren, even if a man is caught in any trespass, you
> who are spiritual, restore such a one in a spirit of
> gentleness; each one looking to yourself, lest you too
> be tempted.

I think obeying authority is becoming one of the most difficult assignments we as Christians have in our society. So often we find that our employers have very different values and beliefs. If they make choices or behave in a way that makes us lose respect for them, it's much harder to work with enthusiasm and excellence. Yet here we have an outstanding opportunity to display Christlikeness. I mentioned the 1 Peter passage about submitting to unjust employers; later Peter goes on to say (3:14-17),

> But even if you should suffer for the sake of right-
> eousness, you are blessed. And do not fear their intim-
> idation, and do not be troubled, but sanctify Christ as
> Lord in your hearts, always being ready to make a
> defense to everyone who asks you to give an account
> for the hope that is in you, yet with gentleness and
> reverence; and keep a good conscience so that in the
> thing in which you are slandered, those who revile
> your good behavior in Christ may be put to shame.

CHAPTER SEVEN

N—No Deception

Commit to telling the truth—
no matter what!

I n December 1987 the *Washington Post Magazine* devoted its year-end issue to "1987: The Year of the Big Lie." On the cover was Joe Isuzu, standing as if at a press conference, boldly proclaiming, "1987 was the best year mankind ever had—and next year's going to be even better." Underneath his words stood this bold disclaimer: "He's lying."

Staff writer Walt Harrington explained the appropriateness of the image: "Joe is the turning of some corner in the American psyche to a place where weary, angry, disgusted people have finally concluded they can't trust anybody, nobody, nada—except maybe their spouse, their mother, and their kids, maybe."[1]

Sad but true. Unfortunately, lying has become a way of life for too many of us. The *Post* took a poll (not a scientific poll) to learn how frequently certain lies were told. The results were instructive.

The most frequent lies had to do with covering up a mistake or misdeed. Ninety-three percent of the 273 randomly-selected adults in the Washington, D.C., sample said that the average person lies sometimes or frequently to cover up something he did wrong. This is easy to believe.

How many times have you promised to send someone a report or a package or a check, only to get distracted and forget. Then one day the phone rings, and the person is irate because he still hasn't received what you promised. At such a moment, it's easy to lie and make excuses. It saves face. But lying compromises your integrity, and that's too great a price to pay, no matter how much pride you save.

Other common lies have to do with avoiding embarrassment or avoiding hurting someone else's feelings. The *Post*'s respondents said that people lie sometimes or frequently ninety-two percent of the time to save face and eighty-nine percent of the time to keep from offending someone else. Imagine that! People are that willing to compromise their integrity just to keep things pleasant emotionally. I can understand why.

Lying happens frequently on résumés, at performance reviews, and in recommendations. I often receive letters from department managers in government and from military officers who complain that they are coerced into going easy on substandard performance (i.e., lying about the performance of an incompetent subordinate) because of fears that negative comments may adversely affect the person's career. No one likes to hurt someone's career, but telling the truth is a higher principle. Furthermore, we need not shoulder the responsibility to help a person avoid the consequences of having a bad attitude, a poor work ethic, or other faults. Besides, no one will ever grow as a person or as a worker unless an evaluator helps him understand that his performance is not up to standard.

I've also noticed how letters of recommendation will compromise the truth about an employee. I question the ethics of firing someone and then turning around and writing a glowing endorsement that enables the individual to get a job—and become a problem for another employer. It's an adult version of what happens in many schools: passing a student who is failing merely to get rid of him. It's a form of deception.

Surprisingly, only sixty-six percent of the *Post*'s sample said that people sometimes or frequently lie to get ahead at work. I suspect that this happens far more often than most people think. Many jobs, for instance, evaluate performance in part on quantitative factors. When I was a pilot, we were graded on the number of hours we had flown. So it became common practice by some to cheat a few minutes on recording the time of their takeoff and the time of their landing. Over a thousand missions, those few minutes could add up to some significant "bonus" hours.

Think how that same principle—"fudging," some people call it; "lying" is what the Bible calls it—can be applied to numerous job situations: expense forms, billable hours, overtime, vacation and sick days, loan interest, fees, quotas. A little here and a little there adds up to a habit of deception.

One way some people choose to get ahead at work is to lie. Salespeople often face this temptation when a customer asks about a particular product. It's an excellent product given the customer's needs. But the salesperson stands to make a significantly larger commission on a related product that would not satisfy those needs as well. The temptation is to lie about the products—to berate the one and oversell the other—in order to make more money from the sale of the inferior one.

A related lie concerns misunderstandings in your favor. One day Bill received a statement from the company holding the mortgage on his house. A computer had printed out a report of mortgage interest to be used in preparing taxes. A copy had been filed with the IRS. The problem was that, due to a computer error, the form showed his entire annual payment as well as the interest as deductible—a hefty sum!

Naturally, Bill contacted the company to correct the problem. He learned that, had he said nothing, the error probably would have gone undetected. It was a fluke in the computer program. Now I suppose some people would think of Bill as foolish to have spoken up. But he felt—rightly—that failing to point out the truth in order to get ahead is just as wrong as telling a boldfaced lie.

I agree. I often have to correct the facts after I'm introduced at a speaking engagement. People have presented me as a Top Gun who flew in the Vietnam War; I never flew over Vietnam, nor did I ever carry ordnance, nor was I Top Gun (that's a Navy designation anyway). I've been introduced as the flight lead for the Thunderbirds, the Air Force's precision team; I've flown in precision formation, but never as a member of the Thunderbirds. I've even been represented as an astronaut, which I never was! It's amazing the misconceptions people have. But I've learned to correct these misimpressions, because honesty demands it. How can I speak on integrity if I know that I've been introduced as someone I'm not? That would be a gross duplicity. Even if it's an unintended mistake, it would be deceptive to leave it uncorrected.

And God hates lying in any form. Proverbs 12:22 says, "Lying lips are an abomination to the LORD, but those who deal faithfully are His delight." As we saw before, there are not many things called an "abomination" in Scripture, but lying is one. God hates lying. In fact, we have a good indication of just how seriously He regards deception in a chilling story from the book of Acts. The Church had just been started, and there was a conversion of thousands of people (Acts 2). Peter and the other apostles were proclaiming the gospel with boldness, and the new believers were growing rapidly. One of the ways they expressed their commitment to Christ and to each other was to meet each other's material needs. Those who had property and money used their wealth to provide for the needs of poorer believers, with the apostles overseeing the distribution of goods (4:32-35). In one particular show of generosity, a noble fellow named Barnabas sold some land and donated the entire profits to the needs of the poor (4:36-37).

A couple named Ananias and Sapphira observed this gesture, as well as the praise and gratitude that the Church no doubt showed him for it. And for whatever reason, they decided to perform a similar act with some land that they owned (5:1-2):

> But a certain man named Ananias, with his wife Sapphira, sold a piece of property, and kept back some of the price for himself, with his wife's full knowledge, and bringing a portion of it, he laid it at the apostles' feet.

You can tell that something is wrong here because the passage begins with the word *but.* The writer is about to draw a contrast between the gracious, unsolicited generosity of Barnabas and the subtle deception of Ananias and Sapphira. The exact nature of their wrong was that they hung onto some of the proceeds, yet represented to the Church that their gift was the entire amount.

We don't know why they did this. Perhaps they wanted to look good in front of the church. Maybe they were jealous of Barnabas. It could be that he was a competitor in the real estate business, and they didn't want him gaining a good reputation in the Church without their gaining one, too. Perhaps they had ambitions for leadership. They may have wanted to look spiritual and generous. Or possibly they had debts to pay, but thought that they would be censured if they used the money instead of donating it to the Church.

Whatever their reason, they had to lie to make it work. Not a big lie, just a tiny lie—a little white lie. In fact, they may not have had to actually say anything untrue. Like Barnabas, just bring in the money, lay it in front of the apostles, tell them it came from a real estate deal, and let everyone draw their own conclusions—which, of course, would be that the gift represented the entire proceeds. Where's the problem in that? Consider how God dealt with them for their dishonesty (Acts 5:3-6):

> But Peter said, "Ananias, why has Satan filled your heart to lie to the Holy Spirit, and to keep back some of the price of the land?
> "While it remained unsold, did it not remain your own? And after it was sold, was it not under your control? Why is it that you have conceived this deed in your heart? You have not lied to men, but to God." And as he heard these words, Ananias fell down and breathed his last; and great fear came upon all who heard of it. And the young men arose and covered him up, and after carrying him out, they buried him.

"Lying lips are an abomination to the LORD" (Proverbs 12:22)! You read the outcome of Ananias's actions and you gain a new appreciation for the meaning of the word *abomination*! In brief, you lie, you die. Apparently, Sapphira hadn't read Proverbs 12:22 recently (Acts 5:7-11):

> Now there elapsed an interval of about three hours, and his wife came in, not knowing what had happened. And Peter responded to her, "Tell me whether you sold the land for such and such a price?" And she

said, "Yes, that was the price."

Then Peter said to her, "Why is it that you have agreed together to put the Spirit of the Lord to the test? Behold, the feet of those who have buried your husband are at the door, and they shall carry you out as well." And she fell immediately at his feet, and breathed her last; and the young men came in and found her dead, and they carried her out and buried her beside her husband. And great fear came upon the whole church, and upon all who heard of these things.

Perhaps this judgment seems unusually harsh. Aren't we glad that God isn't judging deception in quite that manner today? But I think He wanted to impress on the early Church a fundamental principle: that He hates lies, even little white lies. Actually, there are no such creatures in God's estimation. Lies are neither little nor white, they are only lies.

On the other hand, God delights in those who deal faithfully and honestly. He rejoices in them; they bring a smile to His face! Isn't that what you want—to feel the smile of God on your life? You can as you pursue a life of ruthless honesty.

You may want to review the three suggestions given in chapter 5 for how you can cultivate such honesty: (1) commit yourself to truth ahead of time; (2) make amends where necessary for past deception; and (3) review your decisions and statements with others whom you trust. If God detests lying as much as we've seen, then you'll want to make every effort to develop a heart of truth and integrity.

It's high time that we replace Joe Isuzu with John Christian. If people smile at Joe Isuzu because they know he's lying, they should have reason to smile at John Christian because (remarkably) they know he's telling the truth.

How do they know that? Because they know that he follows a God of integrity who never deals falsely. Like Him, John Christian is marked by ruthless, unimpeachable honesty. That's the challenge facing you and me. A challenge placed before us, not just by our culture, but by the Lord Himself (Zechariah 8:16-17):

> "These are the things which you should do: speak the truth to one another; judge with truth and judgment for peace in your gates. Also let none of you devise evil in your heart against another, and do not love perjury; for all these are what I hate," declares the LORD.

NOTE: 1. Walt Harrington, "Revenge of the Dupes," *Washington Post Magazine* (December 1987), page 20.

CHAPTER EIGHT

E—Encourage Conflict Resolution

There's a refreshing alternative to bickering
and bitterness—all it costs is pride.

G enesis records that God created the heavens and the earth, and He placed Adam and Eve over all the creatures, over "every creeping thing that creeps on the earth." You and I work with some of those creeps. Just kidding! But people at work do sometimes act like creeps. We all seem to know at least one person who is difficult to get along with. Many of us know more than one such person. Some people are more than just difficult to get along with—they are impossible! They lie. They cheat. They stab others in the back. They create tension and conflict wherever they go.

Sometimes Christian leaders underestimate how much we have to put up with in the workplace. We hear so much about loving people and feeling compassion for their needs; and we should, we must. But we must never underestimate the amount of evil confronting us as we go to work each day. One of the major areas where that evil comes into play is in our relationships with others.

In this chapter, I want to consider how we deal with difficult people and how we resolve conflicts. Our integrity is on the line when it comes to working out differences, so I want to lay a biblical foundation for conflict resolution and then look at four kinds of conflicts and how to handle them.

THE PRIORITY OF RELATIONSHIPS

The workplace is a very task-oriented environment. It's a place for achievement, for accomplishing objectives, for getting things done. As a result, it's easy to treat people in a very utilitarian way and not value them for who they are, but for what they can do for you. Consequently, relationships can easily become utilitarian as well. People become contacts, human resources, and the payroll. They become a means to an end.

But in God's economy, people are intrinsically valuable, apart from their contribution or performance. As a result, relationships are sacred. They are something God cares about deeply. As His people we should treat others as valuable, too.

In Matthew 22:39, the Lord Jesus says that one of the two foundational commandments of Scripture is, "You shall love your neighbor as yourself." This extends to a host of issues in dealing with people, but in the workplace it means, among other things, that we do all we can to maintain healthy relationships. We should treat people as humans made in God's image, not simply as numbers in a business plan. In other words, we must take relationships very seriously.

An additional section of Scripture describing this dynamic is 1 Corinthians 13, the love chapter. There Paul says that our spirituality, our religion, our moral uprightness, is really hollow if it's not backed up by genuine love for people. The love described there is not a feeling so much as a commitment to do what is best for other people. Again, this implies that relationships are sacred.

At work you are with your second family. It's no coincidence that you are around your coworkers and employer. God has sovereignly placed you in these folks' path to represent Him. For many of your coworkers, you will be the only commercial of what Jesus Christ is all about. They will not care where you go the church or what your beliefs are. But they will watch the way you handle the bumps and bruises of life to see if your life shows any sign of having answers. How you relate to them will be a major factor in their impression of you and of Christ. In many jobs, these people will see more of you than your family will. Before we talk about resolving conflicts, let's look quickly at how you can show love.

First, let your attitude reflect that you like being with the people around you. It could be your smile, taking a coworker to lunch, or being a good listener (although not on company time).

Second, show that you wish the best for them and that you are willing to sacrifice to see that they get the best. Take some time as you drive to work to think about the needs of your coworkers. People can tell whether you really care for them or if you are just doing something nice so they will return the favor.

Cultivating a good relationship builds a base in the relationship. This base must be cared for. Conflicts will tend to erode it. Biblical integrity requires that we do all that is reasonable to rebuild this base if it becomes lost.

It's important to realize though that we're not responsible for other people's behavior, only for our own. So when it comes to conflict resolution, we have to draw a firm line between our responsibility and the response of the person with whom we're in conflict. Romans 12:18 tells us: "If possible, *so far as it depends on you*, be at peace with all men" (emphasis added). Conflicts are inevitable, especially at work. You must do all you can to resolve them. But doing all you can may not bring about peace. A lot depends on the other person, on what he chooses to do on his side of the fence. But that's up to him. Just make sure you mow the grass on your side!

How can you do that? Let's consider four areas of conflict resolution that you'll doubtless face on the job.

IRRITATIONS AND INSULTS

It happens every day. Someone does something irritating.

- Another driver cuts in front of you as you're driving to work, testing your vocabulary.
- A coworker shows up late for a meeting and wastes your limited and valuable time.
- Someone borrows a tool from you and doesn't return it by the time you need it.
- Your secretary misspells a word and makes you look bad.
- Your boss makes a critical remark in front of your peers.

The workplace is not only the place where we contribute, it's also a school where we learn how to practice Christ-like values. It is in just such irritating situations where we can grow.

The most important biblical principle we can apply in trying situations is to be able to sift out the big issues from the little ones. There is a time to complain and stand up for our rights, but for many irritations we simply have to endure them without comment or give only a gentle response. In short, we should have a long fuse!

In James 1:19-20 we read,

> Let everyone be quick to hear, slow to speak, and slow to anger; for the anger of man does not achieve the righteousness of God.

It's normal to feel anger because of irritations. But how you let your anger control your speech or your actions can determine the future of important relationships. Anger is an emotion that can often lead us to a response all out of proportion to what happened. It fuels a rather dark impulse in us to retaliate and make someone pay double for our inconvenience. Paul's words remind us,

> Never pay back evil for evil to anyone. . . . Never take your own revenge, beloved, but leave room for the wrath of God. (Romans 12:17,19)

What so easily happens is that we respond to others with a sharp critical remark that expresses our anger and is designed to punish. This then escalates the conflict to a real fire fight. Perhaps that is why we are admonished to respond to irritation and insults with a gentle response: "A gentle word turns away wrath, but a harsh word stirs up anger" (Proverbs 15:2). This is a verse worth memorizing.

Another way some of us express anger is through what some psychologists call a passive-aggressive response. It is a nonverbal way of getting even. Ignoring the offender, deliberately showing up late for a meeting, and bad-mouthing him to others are just some examples. This form of anger may be even worse than an angry remark. It combines anger out of control with cowardice in not confronting the offender directly. Perhaps this is why the Scriptures praise those with a long fuse: "He who is slow to anger is better than the mighty, and he who rules his spirit, than he who captures a city" (Proverbs 16:32).

One final thought on anger: It not only tempts us to an inappropriate response, but it also causes us to focus on the action of the offender rather than on our own response, which should be primary. No one makes us angry, it is our choice.

So then, what do we do with our feelings of anger? The first thing I do is ask myself why I'm angry. Most of the time it's just my selfishness or pride. If a driver slows me down on my way to a meeting, I'm mad because of the potential embarrassment of being late. Just knowing that diffuses some of my anger. Second, I diffuse anger through simple forgiveness. When I reflect on how much Christ has forgiven me, somehow the big issues and the little issues come into focus.

There are times when it is legitimate to express to someone that you are upset. If you are a boss, you may have to correct an employee. If the problem could affect your whole career, your family's well being, or your company's survival, by all means speak up! But when you do, do it with respect—graciously but in a firm direct manner. Again the book of Proverbs has wisdom for an occasion such as this:

> Like apples of gold in a setting of silver is a word spoken in right circumstances. (Proverbs 25:11)

So when it comes to irritations, separate the big issues from the little ones, and guard the dark side of your anger: "Do not be overcome by evil, but overcome evil with good" (Romans 12:21).

INJUSTICE

A friend of mine once hired a salesman who took a sizable draw against commission, and then left the company before doing a dime's worth of sales. That was a rotten thing to do, and as you can imagine, my friend was pretty upset. He was hurt, he was angry, and he felt ripped off.

When I hear about cases of injustice like that, I just boil. I think Christians should be upset by injustice. But what we do with that anger and how we respond to injustice is *very* important.

Anger in itself is not wrong. In my friend's case, I encouraged him to find the salesman and talk with him. That salesman needed to hear just how angry and hurt his former boss felt in response to his dirty trick. At the same time, the man needed to be confronted with his lack of ethics, and a way needed to be worked out to repay the money.

We just looked at Romans 12—its caution against retaliation and its advice to overcome evil with good. One aspect of promoting good is to seek for a reconciliation in the relationship. That's what my friend did. He confronted the salesman on his shameful behavior, but he also opened the door to reconciliation.

What a contrast this is to a response of bitterness. Bitterness is a deadly poison that destroys us, a weed that chokes the life out of our relationships (see Hebrews 12:15). It's a choice we make to hold onto our anger. We think that by doing so we'll punish the person who has wronged us; we'll get even! Yet the person we hurt the most, and often the only person we hurt at all, is ourself.

By all means, let go of bitterness! You may have been completely wronged. You may be the innocent victim of someone else's terrible, tragic, disgusting choice. You may be permanently scarred because of something someone has done to you. Consequently, you may feel incredible rage and bitterness and a desire to pay that person back. But the counsel of God's Word is *let it go!*

Reconciliation begins with forgiveness. It's so hard to feel forgiving toward someone who has cheated us, especially if we have to live with the long-term consequences of their actions. Yet that is what is so unique about us as Christians: Because we ourselves have been forgiven by God, we can extend forgiveness to others who have wronged us. (See Matthew 18:21-35.) Ephesians 4:32 encourages us, "Be kind to one another, tender-hearted, forgiving each other, just as God in Christ also has forgiven you."

In addition to forgiveness, though, I think we have to seek for justice and try to right whatever wrongs may have been done. I suppose some people would disagree here. Yet I'm not sure that God always requires us to live under the consequences of someone else's moral failure. People need to face accountability for their choices. It's important for them, and for the rest of us, that they be held responsible for their actions. It's hard to read the Old Testament prophets without concluding that just as God values love, He also values justice and righteousness (e.g., Isaiah 1:16-17, Jeremiah 7:5-7, Amos 5:14-15, Zechariah 7:9-10).

This doesn't necessarily mean lawsuits, but it certainly doesn't exclude them. Many Christians wonder whether lawsuits are permissible because of Paul's words in 1 Corinthians 6:1-8. The context has to do with lawsuits between Christians, where one believer goes to court against another believer. It's clear that Paul views such suits as a disgrace. They display disunity in the Church before the world. They place believers in subjection to those who do not know God. And they reveal a breakdown in the way the Church should operate (i.e., Christians should reconcile their differences in a peaceful manner, striving to maintain their relationships with each other and also reach an agreeable, reasonable settlement).

So does Paul categorically rule out lawsuits between

Christians? Yes, I think he teaches that if the issue is just between two believers, they ought to settle the matter outside of the courts. Paul seems to suggest some kind of arbitration by church leaders rather than a lawsuit.

However, not all disputes can be settled by arbitration. Then what? I believe that as believers our preference at that point should be to accept the injustice and move on. As Paul says, "Why not rather be wronged? Why not rather be defrauded?" The reputation of our faith is at stake.

I once hired an itinerant preacher to do some stone work for me. He was a handyman and offered to do the work for less than a normal contractor. So I wrote him a rather large check to buy the materials. Can you believe he skipped town?

I was so angry! I was out a lot of money, so I reviewed all of my options. Eventually I caught up with him, and he refused to pay! I could have hauled him into court and attempted to get my money back, as well as punished him for his misdeed, but on the basis of 1 Corinthians 6, I let it go. That was hard and it cost me a lot, but I felt in conscience it was the right way to handle the situation.

Sometimes there are other people's interests at stake besides your own, or the misdeeds are criminal. Other times, self-protection is at stake. In those cases, we have little recourse but to go to court and press for justice—even though we're pressing charges against a professing believer.

I recall just such a situation. A vice president in a major firm discovered that a manager under him had embezzled money from the company. The manager claimed to be a believer. Naturally, the vice president confronted the man, but he denied the whole thing. At that, the vice president said he would have to press charges. He was shocked when the manager angrily replied, "Press charges! How could you think of such a thing? I thought you were a Christian!"

Feeling rather shaken by the man's protests, the vice president called me to ask whether he might be violating some biblical principle in threatening a suit. After reviewing the situation, I advised that he had to press charges, for three reasons. First, he had a fiduciary responsibility to his company as an officer of the corporation. He had to do what he could to recoup the loss. Second, he needed to show others in the company that behavior of this sort would not be tolerated. Finally, I felt that criminal proceedings would probably be the only way he could get through to this fellow about the seriousness of his actions.

I believe lawsuits should always be a last resort. Like Paul, I think it's a disgrace and a defeat when Christians must resort to that. But we live in an imperfect world where we can't always achieve the ideal.

PERSECUTION

Sometimes I wonder whether we Christians in the West have a right to call the personal shots we take because of our faith "persecution." Usually, the worst we have to face is a raised eyebrow, a verbal slur, or maybe even some mild ostracism. But boy, do we feel traumatized when it happens! Yet for many believers elsewhere around the world—and throughout history—persecution is real and it's serious.

I attended a conference once in Washington, D.C., on Christians behind the Iron Curtain. A pastor from an Eastern Bloc country described what his faith had cost him. He said that the government had learned about his religious activities. So one day when his eight-year-old daughter went to school, the teachers organized an assembly of the entire school in the auditorium, and put her on the stage. Then they began telling her classmates about her father and his silly beliefs, and by these means the teachers worked up the assembly into a chorus of laughter and derision. That little girl had to stand there and take the ridicule because of her father's commitment to Christ. It was a dastardly means of persecution!

As for the father himself, the officials put him through intensive interrogation, psychological abuse, and various techniques of brainwashing. They even gave him drugs to confuse him and break him down. All of this, just because of his faith in Christ!

Many believers face even worse persecution than that man. But certainly not in our culture. Someday, God may allow that in the United States, but for now, we have been spared this trauma. Still, if we're going to be serious about our commitment to Christ, and if we're going to let it make a difference in our lives, we have to expect that we'll face persecution of some sort. In fact, it's promised in 2 Timothy 3:12: "Indeed, all who desire to live godly in Christ Jesus will be persecuted." I should add that along with that promise of persecution is a promise that God will make it up to us someday. Matthew 5:10-12 says,

> "Blessed are those who have been persecuted for the sake of righteousness, for theirs is the kingdom of heaven. Blessed are you when men cast insults at you, and persecute you, and say all kinds of evil against you falsely, on account of Me. Rejoice, and be glad, for your reward in heaven is great, for so they persecuted the prophets who were before you."

The same promises are mentioned in Luke 6:20-23. But in this passage, a sober addition is included (verses 24-26):

> "But woe to you who are rich, for you are receiving your comfort in full. Woe to you who are well-fed

now, for you shall be hungry. Woe to you who laugh now, for you shall mourn and weep. Woe to you when all men speak well of you, for in the same way their fathers used to treat the false prophets."

Persecution, insults, ostracism, and the like for the sake of the gospel hurt and cost us a great deal, but the alternative costs a great deal more. It's a terrible and lonely thing when a doctor is not invited to a party of doctors because of his faith. Or when a construction worker is teased and harassed by others on the crew. Or when a data processor is laughed at or discriminated against by her supervisor because of her spiritual convictions. Or when a homemaker is derided by her unbelieving husband. But think of the alternative: to be liked and admired by the crowd, yet to never be known as a friend of Jesus! That would be a worse tragedy, because it would mean that we had lost our influence for Christ. It could well mean that we had become too much in love with the approval of others. Jesus made it clear that we are to seek His glory, not that of man:

> "How can you believe, when you receive glory from one another, and do not seek the glory that is from the one and only God?" (John 5:44)

How then can we deal with persecution? First, as we have seen, we have to expect it. But second, we have to absorb it with gladness—even though it hurts. Earlier we looked at 1 Peter 4:12-13 in regard to insults. Peter explains that our model for handling persecution is Jesus:

> For you have been called for this purpose, since Christ also suffered for you, leaving you an example for you to follow in His steps, who committed no sin, nor was

any deceit found in His mouth; and while being
reviled, He did not revile in return; while suffering,
He uttered no threats, but kept entrusting Himself to
Him who judges righteously; and He Himself bore
our sins in His body on the cross, that we might die to
sin and live to righteousness; for by His wounds you
were healed. (1 Peter 2:21-24)

When our faith is the reason for being treated with
hostility and injustice, then there is no need to defend
ourselves. Like Christ, we have the opportunity to suffer on
behalf of the gospel.

It will be much easier for us to bear such persecution if
we can disengage ourselves from needing the approval of
others. If we have to have their approval, then we'll be
trapped into pleasing them. And that means we'll compromise our testimony.

MAKING APOLOGIES

Sooner or later you're going to offend someone. Or you're
going to make a mistake. Or you're going to say something
you shouldn't have said. You're likely to lose your temper.
However you do it, sooner or later you're going to cause a
problem in a relationship, and you're going to have to
apologize.

Easier said than done! Some of us would rather lose a
friend, leave a job, split a church, or even incur thousands of
dollars in legal fees than say (with sincerity) two little words:
"I'm sorry!" Is our pride really so great? Apparently it is.

God takes this matter of relationships so seriously that
He tells us not to even bother trying to worship Him until
we've apologized and done what we can to make reconciliation. In Matthew 5:23-24, Jesus said,

"If therefore you are presenting your offering at the altar, and there remember that your brother has something against you, leave your offering there before the altar, and go your way; first be reconciled to your brother, and then come and present your offering."

Do you realize what Jesus is saying? He's painting a picture of a guy in a church. During the service he remembers that he's offended Joe and created a problem in their relationship. So he gets out of his pew in the middle of the sermon, marches up the aisle, goes to his car, drives to Joe's church, walks down the aisle in the middle of the sermon there, finds Joe, pulls him out of his seat, takes him outside, and says, "Joe, I'm sorry! I've made a mistake. I was wrong. I apologize. I hope you'll forgive me!"

They talk awhile and get things worked out. Then they shake hands, and the first man drives back to his church. He gets there just in time for the benediction. But the fact that he missed the sermon doesn't matter. He's just done something more valuable than a year's worth of sermons: he's obeyed God by reconciling himself to his brother.

This sounds extreme, but it's not far from what Christ actually said. I wish we would see more of it. If we literally applied these verses, we'd have traffic jams every Sunday as people commuted between churches to apologize!

The point is this: When we're having conflict with another person, we need to take the initiative to go to that person and apologize, and do whatever we can to clean up the relationship.

ANGER AND RIGHTEOUSNESS

Earlier we looked at James 1:19 about being slow to anger. Unfortunately, some Christians think this means that believers should *never* get angry. But the Bible doesn't teach that. James says be *slow* to anger. Verse 20 goes on to explain why: "For the anger of man does not achieve the righteousness of God." James is reminding us that when we're steamed up over an issue to where anger controls us, we're not likely to respond in a Christlike manner. This is particularly relevant to conflict resolution.

When we're offended by someone's behavior, or insulted by someone's comment, or when someone has treated us unjustly or persecuted us for our faith in Christ, it's natural to feel anger. But it's also easy to lose our objectivity in the process. Anger can cause us to lose perspective to such an extent that we can't evaluate the situation realistically.

For that reason, when we're in conflict with someone, it's especially important to seek the input of others to help us do the right thing and respond in a healthy way. Notice, I didn't say to get other people to side with us so that we can gang up on our opponent and overwhelm him. Rather, we need others who will help us keep things in perspective and encourage us to resolve the conflict appropriately. This will help us avoid rationalizing a reaction of anger that would not achieve a righteous outcome.

It's so important that we resolve conflicts as best we can. After all, the Christian who is weak in relationships is a weak Christian. You see, integrity is more than just having high standards or living a morally correct lifestyle. It also has to do with the way we treat people, and the quality of our love for them. By resolving conflicts, we show that we care for more than the tasks of our careers—we care about people. That's the compassionate side of integrity.

CHAPTER NINE

S—Sexual Fidelity
If you think you're above sexual compromise,
read this chapter!

Perhaps you're familiar with John Molloy's best-selling book *How to Dress For Success.* In this chapter I want to talk about how to *stay* dressed for success! I'll look at how you can preserve your integrity when it comes to sexual temptation.

I suppose right away we might well ask why this should even be an issue that needs discussion. After all, isn't it obvious that sexual immorality is wrong from a biblical point of view? Yes, it is obvious, but that doesn't prevent it from spreading like wildfire! We're terribly naive if we think that just because we condemn adultery and immorality that this alone will keep us pure. Remember the warning of 1 Corinthians 10:12: "Let him who thinks he stands take heed lest he fall."

None of us is above committing sexual immorality. Perhaps it's not the worst of sins, but I think it's very serious *and* very prevalent. In fact, it's on the rise. A study by the Alan Guttmacher Institute and Ortho Pharmaceuticals found that sexual activity among all single women increased five percent between 1982 and 1988 to seventy-six percent.

This, in the face of the AIDS crisis!

In chapter 2, I mentioned Barbara Gutek's findings that as many as thirty-five million Americans have a "sociosexual experience" with a coworker in any given week. Sex at work is a problem, she says, for up to half of all workers—more so for women than for men.

Several reasons for this increase are suggested. First, women have entered the work force in a major way in the last twenty years. Many of those women have taken jobs in traditionally male-dominated fields. Furthermore, since 1954 the work week for the average business or professional person is up twenty percent, which means these workers have less time for social contact outside work and more time than ever on the job with coworkers. The net result is that contacts between the sexes have increased dramatically in the workplace. In addition, relationships in general are increasingly built around work.

Add to this the permissive attitude toward sex that prevails in our culture, the coming of age of the baby boomers who bring with them a casual attitude toward sex, the heightened levels of stress associated with many jobs, the breakdown of traditionally conservative institutions like the family and religion, and you have a society in which sexual impurity is only a choice away.

It *can happen* to you or to me. It *is* happening to millions around us. And it *will* happen to us unless we take very conscious, practical, and biblical steps to prevent it. Let me suggest ten ideas for how to *stay dressed* for success.

Make Up Your Mind that Sexual Immorality Is Wrong, and that Sexual Purity Is Right.

While many of us learned early in our Christian experience that sex outside of marriage is wrong, it's worth reviewing some of the biblical passages on this subject. The place to begin is with God's ideal: one man and one woman united in marriage. Genesis 2:24 reads, "For this cause a man shall leave his father and his mother, and shall cleave to his wife; and they shall become one flesh."

Marriage is God's institution for an intimate relationship between a man and a woman, of which sexual intimacy is a part. Sex is not a sin. It's a healthy, normal, God-ordained act that is to be enjoyed in the confines of a marriage. All sexual liaisons outside that marriage amount to sin. So serious does God view such illicit encounters that in the Old Testament He instructed the Israelites to punish sexual offenders with death (Leviticus 20:10-16).

In the New Testament, the sanctity of marriage is upheld (Matthew 19:4-6, Ephesians 5:25-31). Likewise, all sexual intimacy outside of marriage is condemned (e.g., 1 Corinthians 6:15-20, 1 Thessalonians 4:2-8). In fact, Jesus extended the ideal of sexual purity beyond the physical act itself to the thoughts of a person (Matthew 5:27-28). In short, sexual immorality of any kind is opposed to God's will (Ephesians 5:1-4).

Practically speaking, then, this means that if you are married and you are sexual with anyone who is not your spouse, you are sinning. If you are married and you are sexual with a single person, you are sinning. If you are single and you are sexual with another single person or with a married person, you are sinning. There are no doubt many psychological and sociological factors involved here as well, but here is the bottom line from Scripture: Sex was intended for married couples; sex apart from marriage is wrong.

It would be hard if not impossible for a person to attain to any level of sexual purity if he can't agree to this. I realize that there are many views about sex in our culture that conflict with this teaching. But what determines the morality of your sexual thoughts and behavior should not be the ideas of your psychologist, your parents, Dr. Ruth, or even your own feelings, but rather the Word of God. Though many disagree with Him, He says that sexual purity is right and sexual immorality is wrong.

Decide that You'll Fulfill Your Sexual Needs in a Healthy Way in Marriage.

Sex is a normal, healthy part of being human. So it's important that you express your sexuality in a healthy way. That means, first, deciding that marriage is the only relationship where you'll pursue sexual intimacy.

Obviously sexuality extends beyond marriage. It's inevitable that somewhere along the way you'll be attracted physically, emotionally, and sexually to someone besides your spouse. It would be naive and unrealistic to think otherwise. But Scripture warns us sternly against acting on that attraction. One preventive step is to decide ahead of time that the only place where you'll allow your sexual drives to proceed unchecked is alone with your spouse.

First Corinthians 7:3-5 tells us,

> Let the husband fulfill his duty to his wife, and likewise also the wife to her husband. The wife does not have authority over her own body, but the husband does; and likewise also the husband does not have authority over his own body, but the wife does. Stop depriving one another, except by agreement for a time that you may devote yourselves to prayer, and come together again lest Satan tempt you because of your lack of self-control.

It's interesting that Paul actually commands married couples to engage in sex. If you're single and have never been married, you may wonder why that would be necessary! I'll speak about issues relevant to singles in a moment. The reality is that the familiarity of marriage so often breeds a degree of contempt or distance between the partners, as the flaws and foibles of each are exposed. Unless you take active steps to work through these barriers, your sexual relationship will suffer. In a real sense, the quality of your sexual life with your wife or husband is a good indicator of the quality of your overall relationship.

If you don't have your sexual needs fulfilled with your spouse, you'll likely seek to have them met elsewhere. That's why it's so crucial that you cultivate a healthy marriage of which sex is a vital part. The next two suggestions will help you do that.

Watch Out for Overwork and Emotional Exhaustion.
The main work ethic today is the ethic of *careerism*: people let work determine and define their lives. As a result, many are putting in incredible hours on the job, which obviously means that they have little time left for spouses and families. What's worse, whether their jobs take five percent or eighty-five percent of their time, many pour ninety-five percent of their emotional energy into their work. That means they have nothing left in those few hours when they do come home.

Living that way, we put ourselves in grave danger of sexual vulnerability. If we want to maintain integrity in this area, we need to balance our time and our use of emotional energy. Bill and I have written on this problem in *How to Balance Competing Time Demands* (NavPress, 1989). We suggest that biblically you have a responsibility to honor God in five major areas of life: your personal life, marriage and family, work, church, and community.

Notice that work is only one of five areas. If all of your energy is going into your job, you're not honoring God with your life. Obviously, work is an important part of life, but God wants us to pursue faithfulness to Him in the other four areas as well. That means that you'll have to strike a strategic balance among these various areas—a balance of time commitments and a balance in the use of your emotional energy.

By the way, you need to be especially on guard here if you have children. Your job will take a lot out of you, and your kids will demand even more. You therefore face a greater danger of neglecting your spouse and his or her needs—and even more, your own needs.

Take Care for Where Your Needs for Significance and Emotional Intimacy Are Met.

There's no question that work can be a challenging, fulfilling, and emotionally captivating experience. It's not always that way, but for many of us, work is the place where we prove ourselves and show what we can do. Consequently, it's natural to feel a real bond with our coworkers. They know better than anyone what it takes to get the job done and what it means when we do.

That's as it should be. But there's a potential danger when the people affirming us and giving us approval are members of the opposite sex. The tremendous feelings of acceptance and understanding can make others look very attractive—especially if we're unsatisfied with things at home.

I know a man who is in mid-life, facing all the normal things men at that age face: fears about his sexual potency, concerns about his appearance, questions about the value of his work. He has real emotional needs right now. Unfortunately, his wife is too wrapped up in getting her kids off to college to pay him much attention.

This man works sixty or sixty-five hours a week, in a

very responsible position. In fact, he's at work more than he's at home. That means he spends more time interacting with his secretary and other women at work than he does with his wife. I think he's very vulnerable to sexual temptation.

After all, the women at work do their best to look attractive and professional. They pay him respect. They ask his opinion. They listen. They help him with problems and projects. They joke with him and laugh at his jokes. They discuss important matters. And they work hard with him to achieve goals and accomplish tasks. In many ways they are closer to him emotionally and personally than his wife.

That's a dangerous situation, one that you and your spouse will want to take care to avoid. If you're a husband, you need to work at listening to your wife to understand her feelings and expressing your own emotions as well. If you're a wife, you need to encourage your husband and treat him with respect. Ask him not only about the nature of his work, but his emotions about it, too.

Sexual infidelity almost always begins with emotional infidelity first. Don't let that happen to you! Cultivate a healthy relationship with your spouse built on affirmation, emotional honesty, and trust.

Don't Flirt with Danger.

Remember the naive young fool in Proverbs 7? He was literally seduced into sexual immorality because he placed himself squarely in the path of the prostitute. The same can happen to you and me if we toy with sexual temptation. As Proverbs 6:27-28 warns:

> Can a man take fire in his bosom,
> And his clothes not be burned?
> Or can a man walk on hot coals,

And his feet not be scorched?
So is the one who goes in to his neighbor's wife;
Whoever touches her will not go unpunished.

Obviously we need to avoid actual flirtation with the opposite sex. We also need to avoid situations that could easily lead us to compromise. For instance, meetings with a member of the opposite sex in a hotel room, a home, or anywhere when no one else is present, are obviously unwise. While nothing may necessarily happen, there's surely nothing to prevent it. A good rule of thumb is this: What would this situation *look like* if viewed by someone who did not know the context? What would it look like to my spouse? We actually have biblical precedent for this. Romans 13:13-14 exhorts,

> Let us behave properly as in the day, not in carousing and drunkenness, not in sexual promiscuity and sensuality, not in strife and jealousy. But put on the Lord Jesus Christ, and make no provision for the flesh in regard to its lusts.

Along the same lines, be very careful about physically touching members of the opposite sex. As 1 Corinthians 7:1 says, "Now concerning the things about which you wrote, it is good for a man not to touch a woman."

Sure, some people are very friendly and come from families where hugs, kisses, hand holding, and the like were a part of life. But you have to be very careful about touch, for it is a powerful means of communication. It breaks the natural, invisible barriers that most of us assume, and invades another's space. Touch can so easily be taken the wrong way and lead to the wrong consequences.

Another one of your senses to guard is your eye-gate:

Watch what you watch! Be very critical of the movies you attend, the television shows you watch, and the magazines and books you pick up. I'm not suggesting that you be a prude or that you become neurotic about any photo with flesh in it. Just remember the warning of 1 John 2:16 about the "lust of the eyes." I suggest you take active steps to eliminate from your visual diet whatever material stimulates lust and fantasies for you.

One final caution: *Beware when alcohol is present!* I'm not going to comment here on whether Christians should or shouldn't use alcohol. It's a fact that alcohol is in frequent use among people in the work world in a variety of settings. If you choose to partake, keep in mind that it is a depressant that lowers inhibitions and makes it harder to think straight. That can create obvious problems if you're suddenly confronted with sexual temptation.

The overall attitude we need to adopt in the area of flirting with sexual temptation is expressed in Romans 13:14: "Put on the Lord Jesus Christ, and make no provision for the flesh in regard to its lust."

Set High Standards for Your Dating Relationships.
I don't envy singles today in the least. I see incredible pressures placed on them, and sexual pressures lead the pack. In many groups, it's expected that an evening's outing will end up in bed. That can leave you very lonely and dismayed if you don't want to give in to that.

Let me challenge you, if you're single, to set and hold on to godly standards for your dating life. I caution you to think carefully before dating a person who does not know Christ or is uncommitted to Him. After all, every dating relationship is a potential marriage relationship. Trust me, you don't want to go through life with someone who has no regard for the Lord.

I would also caution singles against any sort of sexual intimacy beyond kissing and hugging. You'll have to decide where to draw the line. But don't let either internal or external pressures drive you down a road of moral compromise.

Safeguard Yourself Against Temptation.

Traveling puts you in one of the most vulnerable positions there is when it comes to sexual compromise. You're in unfamiliar surroundings. Often you're physically tired and emotionally spent. There are none of the usual barriers holding you back from sexual behaviors. Perhaps no one will know if you give in to temptation.

It's important to take practical steps to prevent immorality. You know yourself, so you can devise an appropriate plan for you. But I suggest that you "check in" on the phone with your spouse every day, perhaps even twice a day. Don't just say hello and good-bye, but talk about your day and your spouse's day, your needs and hers.

Also, plan your use of time. Boredom is a climate in which immorality flourishes. So stock up on worthwhile reading material. Or tour the area you're visiting, and use your mind to think about its history, its significance, its way of life, and its cultural uniqueness. You might also plan ahead to visit friends or relatives who happen to live in the area.

One of the things to decide ahead of time is that you'll avoid the movies that are cabled into your hotel room. Likewise, avoid situations where you're alone with the opposite sex. And as I said earlier, beware when alcohol is present.

Pray that You'll Maintain Your Sexual Purity.

The 1 Corinthians 7 passage that we looked at earlier spoke of the importance of keeping your sex life healthy, "lest

Satan tempt you." Likewise, 1 Peter 3:7 encourages husbands to care for their wives, "so that your prayers may not be hindered." There's a definite connection between your prayer life and your sex life.

By praying to maintain your sexual purity, and inviting your spouse to do the same, what I have in mind is that you solicit God's strength to help you stay clean. Sexual temptation, after all, is a spiritual matter and ultimately requires spiritual resources to overcome. If you and your spouse both make this area a matter of prayer, you unleash God's power to help you do what is right. You also build intimacy by joining together to overcome a mutual enemy.

When You Face Raw Temptation, Flee!
Second Timothy 2:22 says,

> Now flee from youthful lusts, and pursue righteousness, faith, love and peace, with those who call on the Lord from a pure heart.

As you confront various kinds of evil in life, there's a time to stand your ground and fight, and there's a time to run away. When you're confronted by a clear, unquestionable solicitation to compromise your sexual morality, it's time to run away.

Our model in this regard is Joseph. In Genesis 39 we read the story of Joseph as a manager over a government official's household and related matters. The official's wife became sexually attracted to this competent young man, and hounded him day after day to have sex with her. But he refused, and it would appear that there were various safeguards in place to assist him in resisting her.

One day Joseph was alone in the house with her. On that occasion, she physically grabbed him. But he pulled away with such force that he left his cloak in her hands. To maintain his integrity, he literally tore out of his clothes and fled the house.

Would you leave your coat behind to get away from an invitation to compromise? I think we need to be prepared to do that as we live and work in our society. It's altogether possible that someday, when we least expect it, a coworker will make it plain that he or she wants to have sex with us. When that moment arrives, we have but one alternative: *flee!*

Never Forget the Consequences of Immorality.
I have never talked with a person who has committed sexual immorality who did not share the experience with tears in his eyes. Those few moments of pleasure have set him on a lifetime of regret and grief.

There's no question, of course, that God can and does forgive us for sexual failures, just as He does any other sin. And we hope that we can be restored to those whom we have wronged. Nevertheless, sexual compromise is a sin that seems to have permanent repercussions.

I could fill a book with the tragic stories of men and women who have seen their marriages, children, friendships, businesses, careers, and the rest of what matters to them vaporized by a lapse of sexual integrity. As Proverbs 6:32 puts it:

> The one who commits adultery with a woman is
> lacking sense;
> He who would destroy himself does it.

Immorality causes severe, permanent damage. By contrast, sexual purity leads to health and life. If you want to feel the smile of God upon your life and to live with confidence and a clean conscience, pursue integrity in this area. It's the path of wisdom, where there are no regrets.

> Now therefore, O sons, listen to me,
> For blessed are they who keep my ways.
> Heed instruction and be wise,
> And do not neglect it.
> Blessed is the man who listens to me,
> Watching daily at my gates,
> Waiting at my doorposts.
> For he who finds me finds life,
> And obtains favor from the LORD.
> But he who sins against me injures himself;
> All those who hate me love death. (Proverbs 8:32-36)

CHAPTER TEN

T—Trustworthiness

*Most people make contingency commitments,
but you can stand out
as a person of your word.*

Integrity is ultimately a matter of trust. If you're a person of integrity, it means people know that they can rely on you to do the right thing in matters of responsibility and morality. So rounding out our discussion of the principles of integrity is the quality of trustworthiness.

I have to tell you that I have something of an ax to grind in this area. I'm shocked and angered as I see Americans in general and Christians in particular abandoning this virtue. More and more people are adopting very self-seeking attitudes toward life, and placing ultimate value on their own self-fulfillment. As a result, they can't really be trusted to do what they say they'll do; the only thing you can count on is that they'll do what is best for them.

In other words, people now make contingency commitments: they'll agree to something, until something better comes along. I think, for instance, of a lawyer who will take on a small case, and then put it on the shelf when a bigger, more lucrative case comes along. Or a salesman who baits the customer with one promise, only to switch to a different arrangement once he detects interest. Or a contractor who promises to fix certain problems in a new house during the walk-through, but who never sends anyone back to do the work.

We can all think of situations where someone hasn't followed through on their word. I almost expect this from people who do not know God or do not love Him. But what really frosts me are the many instances when Christians break their commitments.

A man in a certain city signed a contract to buy a building from an eighty-year-old woman. This woman had held onto the property as an investment, and now she needed to sell it to help provide for her needs in her final years. The man was a well-known Christian in that town, who gave a lot of money to Christian causes and was outspoken in his faith, the sort of man every Christian organization would love to have on its board.

Finally, it came time to close on the deal. The woman met with her lawyers and his lawyers to sign everything and transfer the money. A friend of mine was in the room. He told me that after everyone was assembled, the man marched into the room and announced, "I've changed my mind. I've found something else I'd rather invest in. I'm not interested in your building."

"But what about the contract?" he was asked.

"It's off. You can sue me if you want!" And he walked out of the room.

My friend was so shocked by this that he called me immediately, just to get some perspective. I don't know that I was much help, because I was outraged! I still get angry just thinking about it! Imagine the disrepute brought on the cause of Christ because of that man's lack of trustworthiness. I can just hear people in the business community in his town chortling: "Sure, he's a religious man, but he's a businessman first and foremost. He's a do-gooder, all right, but when push comes to shove he's as much of a snake as the rest of us!"

I'm afraid this kind of behavior is becoming all too common among Christians, but it's totally opposed to the teaching of Scripture. If you're going to keep your ethical edge sharp, then you need to decide up front that you'll be a trustworthy person. Let's consider what that means.

FAITHFULNESS AND RELIABILITY

As we trace the concept of trustworthiness through the Scriptures, we find that it has two edges to it. First of all, it involves keeping your word even if it becomes inconvenient. This is the idea of *faithfulness*. In chapter 3 we looked at Psalm 15, where the psalmist asks who gets to enjoy an intimate, satisfying relationship with God. The answer is that it's the person with integrity. In verse 4 of the psalm, we find that one of the characteristics of the person of integrity is, "He swears to his own hurt, and does not change."

In other words, when the trustworthy person signs his name on an agreement, it's a done deal; he's not going to change his mind if something better comes along. In Psalm 15 we see this kind of faithfulness at work in the business world. It is no less important in spiritual commitments. Ecclesiastes 5:4-5 warns us:

> When you make a vow to God, do not be late in paying it, for He takes no delight in fools. Pay what you vow! It is better that you should not vow than that you should vow and not pay.

In addition to faithfulness, though, the biblical concept of trustworthiness also involves *reliability*—that is, fulfilling our responsibilities. Apparently this has been a problem since Solomon's day, for in Proverbs 20:6 he says, "Many a man proclaims his own loyalty, but who can find a trustworthy man?"

In other words, everyone tells you he's dependable, but where is he when there's work to do? Perhaps, like me, you've felt this way when you've taken your car to a garage and are told it'll be ready that day, but when you return you discover that they can't get to it until tomorrow at the earliest!

Such unreliability is really akin to incompetence. Proverbs 18:9 says, "He also who is slack in his work is brother to him who destroys." Does this verse convict you the way it convicts me? It implies that excellence should be the hallmark of my work, that no one should have to look over my shoulder to make sure I get the job done. Furthermore, it suggests that if I am negligent in fulfilling my responsibilities, I might as well be actively destroying my work.

In short, biblical trustworthiness means that when I'm given a task or commit to doing one, I follow through on the assignment to the best of my ability, sticking with it until it's done and done right. If that's not a part of my "workstyle," then I really can't say I'm a person of integrity.

A CASE STUDY IN TRUSTWORTHINESS

As we look at the challenges of faithfulness and reliability, an excellent case study is in the book of 1 Samuel. There we find the story of Israel's first king, Saul, who was given an important assignment by God. Let's pick up the narrative at the point where Samuel, the prophet of God, explains what Saul is to do (15:3):

> "Now go and strike Amalek and utterly destroy
> all that he has, and do not spare him; but put to

death both man and woman, child and infant, ox
and sheep, camel and donkey."

Amalek refers to the Amalekites, wicked enemies of
Israel who caused God's people no end of trouble. For years
they had been a thorn in the side, and now God was ready to
judge them once and for all by eliminating them from the
earth. It was Saul's job to lead the army against the Amalekites and completely, utterly destroy them—to wipe them
off the face of the earth.

This sounds pretty severe, and we could discuss why
God would deal so harshly with a nation. But the point we
want to look at here is that God gave a specific responsibility
to Saul, a task for which he was well suited, and he did not
balk. First Samuel 15:4-6 records,

Then Saul summoned the people and numbered
them in Telaim, 200,000 foot soldiers and 10,000 men
of Judah. And Saul came to the city of Amalek, and set
an ambush in the valley. And Saul said to the Kenites,
"Go, depart, go down from among the Amalekites, lest
I destroy you with them; for you showed kindness to
all the sons of Israel when they came up from Egypt."
So the Kenites departed from among the Amalekites.

Clearly Saul is ready to strike the Amalekites. He
removes the innocent Kenites, and then gives the order to
attack. Here's what happens (15:7-9):

So Saul defeated the Amalekites, from Havilah as you
go to Shur, which is east of Egypt. And he captured
Agag the king of the Amalekites alive, and utterly
destroyed all the people with the edge of the sword.
But Saul and the people spared Agag and the best of

the sheep, the oxen, the fatlings, the lambs, and all that was good, and were not willing to destroy them utterly; but everything despised and worthless, that they utterly destroyed.

Backed by the power of God, Saul is victorious and carries out God's awesome instructions—*sort of.* I think you can understand why he might overlook the choicest of the animals. It would be somewhat like God telling you to go in and liquidate a competitor who had cheated you for years, to totally empty out his warehouse. You'd go in and start auctioning off various pieces of merchandise. But if you saw particular items that really caught your fancy, you'd be pretty tempted to set those aside for yourself. It's only human nature.

Apparently, though, God wasn't impressed by Saul's choice. According to verses 10-11,

Then the word of the LORD came to Samuel, saying, "I regret that I have made Saul king, for he has turned back from following Me, and has not carried out My commands." And Samuel was distressed and cried out to the LORD all night.

You'll rarely find sadder words in Scripture than when God says, "I regret." Imagine bringing regret and grief to the heart of God! But that's what Saul's lack of faithfulness—his disobedience—brought about. Let's see how the matter ends (verse 12):

And Samuel rose early in the morning to meet Saul; and it was told Samuel, saying, "Saul came to Carmel, and behold, he set up a monument for himself, then turned and proceeded on down to Gilgal."

Saul was so pleased with his victory that he wasted no time in setting up a monument to himself to celebrate. When Samuel arrived, notice what Saul claimed (verse 13): "I have carried out the command of the LORD." Is this true? Hardly! His statements make Saul sound like a child making excuses when caught with his hand in the cookie jar. The evidence against him is insurmountable as the passage shows (verse 14): "But Samuel said, 'What then is this bleating of the sheep in my ears, and the lowing of the oxen which I hear?'"

Now Saul begins a series of excuses to evade responsibility (verse 15):

And Saul said, "They have brought them from the Amalekites, for the people spared the best of the sheep and oxen, to sacrifice to the LORD your God; but the rest we have utterly destroyed."

This is a lie and a joke. Saul blames the people, and at the same time invents the fabrication about sacrifices; then he tries to make his partial obedience stand for the whole. Later, he goes on (verses 21-23):

"But the people took some of the spoil, sheep and oxen, the choicest of the things devoted to destruction, to sacrifice to the LORD your God at Gilgal."
    And Samuel said,
    "Has the LORD as much delight in burnt offerings
        and sacrifices
    As in obeying the voice of the LORD?
    Behold, to obey is better than sacrifice,
    And to heed than the fat of rams.
    "For rebellion is as the sin of divination,
    And insubordination is as iniquity and idolatry.

Because you have rejected the word of the LORD,
He has also rejected you from being king."

There's no substitute for obedience. No amount of religious activity or ritual can substitute for complete obedience to God. Reliability is a part of this obedience. When God gives us an assignment, He expects it to be carried out in full. The principle here relates to trustworthiness. Let me mention two lessons we can learn from Saul's tragic failure.

First, *our trustworthiness is a good measure of our spirituality.* The extent to which we follow through on our commitments says volumes about our fundamental commitment to Christ. That's why faithfulness is listed as one characteristic of the fruit of the Spirit in Galatians 5:22-23. The person who is faithful is demonstrating the Spirit's control over his life. By contrast, the person who falls down on the job, as Saul did, shows that he is not giving God control.

Not long ago a Christian ministry in Dallas held a banquet to raise its visibility in the community and to solicit financial help for its programs. I know this ministry and can vouch for its worthiness. It is doing an outstanding job, but could do an even better job if financed properly. Apparently others felt the same way, because about five hundred reservations were made to attend the banquet.

Now you may know that, at a fundraising event like this, the sponsoring organization usually pays for dinner, figuring the gifts given will cover not only the costs but also help support the ministry. That was the case when this banquet was planned.

Unfortunately for the ministry, though, the Dallas Mavericks basketball team happened to go into the playoffs and played an unscheduled game on the same night as the banquet. It was a scheduling conflict that no one could have foreseen weeks before when arrangements had been set up. Nevertheless, five hundred reservations had been made. Would you believe that a hundred and fifty people didn't show up; presumably they went to the game instead!

I'm sure the leaders of that organization felt cheated. I know I felt they were. People had made a verbal commitment to be at a certain place at a certain time; but later when something better came along, they felt their word could easily be discarded. That ministry had to "eat" a hundred and fifty dinners that night!

Is that what it means to be trustworthy, to live with biblical integrity? Of course not! I like a good basketball game as much as anyone. But if I give my word to show up at a banquet, or at my child's soccer game or birthday party, or anywhere else, then I had better not cancel to attend a basketball game. If I do, I show that I'm really not letting God have control in my life, that I think His standards of trustworthiness don't apply to me. Instead, my only concern is with whatever I want to do.

A second lesson from Saul's life goes hand in hand with this: *Partial obedience is not obedience.* Recall how Saul kept trying to persuade Samuel that he had carried out the assignment, even though he had spared Agag the king and some of the livestock. Saul failed to consider that God's assignment was not partial destruction of Amalek, but total annihilation. God had been very specific about that; He expected complete obedience to the entire plan.

I'm amazed at how impartially people fulfill their assignments in the workplace today. Likewise, they often give only token compliance with standards and regulations.

An example of this is if you're a flight attendant, and you're pregnant. Your employer has definite guidelines about working past a certain point in a pregnancy, but you keep working several weeks past that termination date. At the same time, you actively share your faith with the other flight attendants, and give testimony to the wonderful changes God has brought about in your life.

Can you see the inconsistency? It's great that you want to share the gospel, but that's only partial obedience. It's duplicity and a breach of integrity to keep flying against company policy. You're taking away with your right hand what you're giving with your left.

Return to the banquet and the no-shows: I suppose someone could say, "Well, maybe it was wrong for those people to just not show up. But suppose they called ahead of time to cancel, or maybe even sent in a donation to pay for the meal plus a little something extra for the ministry. That would have been okay, right?"

I think that would have been considerate. But I still think there's an element of partial faithfulness there. You see, by committing to come they were agreeing to do more than just hear a fundraising appeal. They were agreeing to learn more about that ministry, to hear about what God was doing through it, and to meet some of its leaders. So sending in money in lieu of showing up still has a hollow ring to it. It goes against the spirit of making your word your bond.

How, then, can you live and work with genuine trustworthiness? In contrast to Saul, how can you fulfill your responsibilities in a way that maintains godly integrity?

Be Careful What You Promise!

God obviously takes your commitments seriously; so should you. God Himself holds you responsible for the promises you make, both to Him and to others. This being the case, you should not be too quick to make agreements.

Being careful will be especially difficult if you're a person who has a hard time saying no. It may be that you're afraid of disappointing people. Whatever the reason, you should take steps to overcome this habit, because it will ruin your integrity if you can't follow through. You will become so busy trying to get everything done that you'll end up pleasing no one and doing your work poorly—and breaking commitments.

Before you take on a task or engagement, ask yourself: Is this something I need to do? Is it what I want to do? What else in my schedule will I drop in order to take on this responsibility? If it involves money, am I in a financial position that I can afford it? If I fail, what will be the consequences? Is this something that someone else should be doing? Is this the best use of my time and resources? What exactly will my participation in this involve? What does my family think? Bombarding your choices with questions like these can help you sift out the true nature of what you're agreeing to. It will also clarify whether the request or opportunity is worth your involvement.

If you struggle with saying no, then say yes by responding, "This sounds like a great opportunity, but I need to reflect on it before agreeing to get involved. If I do participate, I'll want to give it the attention it deserves. But I need to think about whether I'll be able to do that." Delaying your response can buy you time to think clearly and not rush into making promises you can't keep.

Commit Yourself to Excellence of Effort Rather than Excellence of Results.

Earlier I stressed the importance of doing your work with excellence, and of doing your best to get the job done. This is a part of biblical integrity, but there's a balance to be struck here. One could take this principle of excellence to an unhealthy extreme and become a workaholic, striving to achieve perfection.

Biblically, though, the excellence that God asks us to

pursue is excellence of effort, not excellence of results. In our book *How to Succeed Where It Really Counts* (NavPress, 1989), Bill and I explain that true success before God means faithfully pleasing Him with the resources and responsibilities He's given us. We find this principle in the parable of the talents in Matthew 25.

In that passage, three slaves, or managers, are given five units of money, two units, and one unit, respectively, by their master to invest while he is away. When he returns, the first manager shows him that he has doubled his five talents into ten. Likewise, the second manager doubles his two talents into four. The master praises both these managers and rewards them similarly, even though the first made more money than the second.

The principle is that God rewards us on the basis of our faithfulness, not on the basis of our products. He expects excellence of effort, even when excellence of results eludes us. After all, so much outside our control can keep us from the results we'd like: the decisions of other people, the failures of key participants, the stock market, the economy in general, the weather. There are a host of factors beyond our control that may prevent us from achieving our objectives.

Fortunately, God evaluates us on the basis of the effort we apply in His service—the extent to which we're faithful (even if we're not "successful" from a human standpoint) with the resources and responsibilities He's given us. That means we can set limits on our lives. We can be loyal, dependable employees, doing the best job possible, without having to worry about doing everything perfectly.

Use Extreme Caution in Contracts and Partnerships.
Business inevitably involves contractual obligations. Trustworthiness—fulfilling your commitments no matter what—has real implications for the contracts you enter into. When-

ever you sign your name to an agreement, you're obligating yourself—both as an individual and as a follower of Christ— to abide by the terms and conditions spelled out in the agreement.

Needless to say, you should use extreme caution before signing anything. You should use the same caution before entering into any business arrangement, such as forming a partnership, where you aren't completely confident of all the participants' trustworthiness. That's why Scripture discourages legal commitments with unbelievers. Because they do not serve the Lord, you can never be sure of their ultimate values. Paul warns (2 Corinthians 6:14-18):

> Do not be bound together with unbelievers; for what partnership have righteousness and lawlessness, or what fellowship has light with darkness? Or what harmony has Christ with Belial, or what has a believer in common with an unbeliever? Or what agreement has the temple of God with idols? For we are the temple of the living God; just as God said,
> "I will dwell in them and walk among them;
> And I will be their God, and they shall be My people.
> Therefore, come out from their midst and be separate," says the Lord.
> "And do not touch what is unclean;
> And I will welcome you.
> And I will be a father to you,
> And you shall be sons and daughters to Me,"
> Says the Lord Almighty.

I don't think this passage automatically precludes doing business on the same team with an unbeliever; that would require us to work only with and for Christians. But it clearly warns us against getting our affairs so intertwined with those of unbelievers that we lose control over the ethical direction of the partnership. I think the same principle applies to dealing with believers who no longer walk with God.

Of course, the issue of contracts and our faithfulness in fulfilling them raises this question: Is bankruptcy permissible from a biblical perspective? While the Bible doesn't discuss bankruptcy as such, it sets forth certain principles of integrity that should guide us in thinking through the issue.

The fundamental principle, of course, is that we are to pay back borrowed money, no matter how inconvenient. I know that some people argue that Christians shouldn't borrow money, but I don't find the Scriptures to be that clearly against it. Rather, they discourage us from going into debt, and caution us that if we do borrow money or accept financial liability, we must be prepared to pay it back. This is the spirit, for example, of Proverbs 22:26-27:

> Do not be among those who give pledges, Among those who become sureties for debts.
> If you have nothing with which to pay,
> Why should he take your bed from under you?

Even so, it's quite possible for a businessman to have an inventory of goods and a payroll to pay, and to have done nothing wrong, yet the market suddenly collapses under him. He finds himself in trouble with his creditors, and perhaps things just get worse. What should he do?

Biblically, he needs to commit himself to paying off his obligations as best he can. I know a man who sold his house, all of his furniture, and his car to pay off a debt. That demonstrates incredible integrity.

How different that is from another man who signed up

dozens of well-heeled investors in limited partnerships on real estate deals. When the market collapsed, he promptly took steps to shelter his personal assets, filed for bankruptcy, and moved to another state—leaving investors, partners, employees, and vendors to sort out the mess. Last I heard, it's still in litigation. Meanwhile, this fellow—who was well-known in the Christian community—has started over in his new locale. As far as I'm concerned, that's a total breach of integrity and a disgrace to the name of Christ.

Obviously, though, there are cases where one simply cannot pay back the entire liability. In many partnerships, the partners are "joint and severally liable," such that even if the other partners cannot pay, you as a partner would be liable for the whole. It's unwise to enter into such an arrangement unless you can carry the whole liability. In addition, you should take extreme precautions to know who the other players are, and whether they plan to and are able to hold up their end of the deal.

But realistically, you can find yourself facing obligations that you can never pay off. What should you do? The law has provided protection from creditors in the various forms of bankruptcy. So you could file for bankruptcy in order to protect your assets. Or you could sell everything you have to satisfy at least some of the debt, and then file for bankruptcy. Which option you choose is a matter of conscience. You'll have to decide how much of your future wages you'll want to pledge toward long-term satisfaction of the debt. Seen this way, bankruptcy becomes a legal way to structure your payments as best you can.

What shows a lack of integrity, though, is the manipulation of your assets to protect them from creditors and avoid repaying what you owe. It's common, for instance, for a businessman in trouble to transfer most of his wealth to his wife or children and to buy an expensive home to protect it all from creditors. If you were one of the creditors, imagine how that person's failure to accept responsibility would make you feel!

I can't say that bankruptcy is immoral, or that a believer should never resort to it, but it should be the *last* resort. The Bible is so clear about paying people what you owe. It's a key measure of your integrity.

I've mentioned many instances in which people have skipped out on their commitments. Does anyone ever fulfill their word? You bet! Ed and Rex are two guys who really take this matter of trustworthiness seriously. I know that if they agree to something, it's as good as done.

Several years ago, they decided to sell an unusually successful business in the food service industry, which they had started from scratch and built into a highly respected chain. They located a buyer and, after negotiating, signed a letter of intent to sell, pending the final disposition of a few minor details. This was on a Friday.

On Saturday Ed got a call from an old acquaintance who had heard about the sale and whose company was keenly interested in making an offer. When this man heard that they had already agreed to sell, he offered them $15 million more than the other prospective buyer. Since theirs was a privately held company, Ed and Rex could have pocketed that amount.

The offer sounded attractive, and the man wouldn't take no for an answer. So Ed promised to think about it and call him on Monday. The rest of that weekend, he and Rex and their wives prayed, asking the Lord what they should do. It really didn't take them long to come to the unanimous conclusion: They would honor their commitment to the initial buyer.

On Monday morning, Ed called the second buyer and told him no. As Christians, he said, they had to keep their word, no matter what it might cost them. So they sold their company to the first buyer—and "lost" $15 million.

But that's not the end of the story. The sale was structured so that Ed and Rex would profit from any increase in the value of the company's stock as a result of the sale. Well, the stock did increase. When it was all counted, the partners netted an additional $16 million from the deal! In a literal sense, their integrity paid off.

Obviously, things don't always work out that way. Sometimes keeping our word costs us dearly. But we can't let the cost get in the way of doing what is right.

Being a person of your word and following through with responsibility will yield you a good reputation. But not only that, it will set an example at work and for the next generation—who will someday look to you for leadership, if not now. It will also help you sleep well at night knowing that you have done an H-O-N-E-S-T day's work!

CHAPTER ELEVEN

Ninety-nine Shades of Gray

What should you do when it seems like there is no one right answer?

S o far in our study of integrity we've dealt mostly with behaviors that are clearly right or wrong: treating others fairly and honestly rather than cheating them; complying with the law rather than flaunting it; telling the truth rather than lying; staying faithful to your spouse rather than committing adultery; fulfilling your word rather than breaking commitments. If only all of life were that simple! If only there were a finite number of do's and don'ts that we could obey and maintain our integrity. If only moral challenges came in a choice of two colors: black or white.

As we all know, the majority of choices come packaged in ninety-nine shades of gray. Rarely are situations completely right or completely wrong; instead, they seem to be a mixture of both. Sometimes it is almost impossible to sort out where "right" ends and "wrong" begins. What's worse, our Christian friends have varying opinions: what is right to one person is wrong to someone else. Then when we turn to the Bible, either we can't find our problem addressed directly, or else we hear differing interpretations about what is written.

All of this can be very frustrating! How can you do what's right if you can't determine what right is? And how can you determine what right is if the Bible doesn't speak to your particular issue? Or what do you do if people who know the Bible differ in how they see it? In short, how do you maintain your integrity when you're dealing with normal ambiguity, what we commonly call "gray areas"?

I think that the ability to handle such gray areas is a mark of moral maturity. It is a fact that the Bible doesn't speak to every detail of life. While some areas have clear moral boundaries, God has determined that many (perhaps most) areas of life will demand choices on our part. As free moral agents, He gives us the right and the responsibility to determine what we're going to do.

I want to help you gain a sharper ability to discern wise moral choices, to cut through the fog that surrounds so many challenges you face and arrive at a decision that has integrity to it. I'll offer principles to consider as you devise a strategy for handling gray areas. Then I want to present four specific situations that are loaded with moral ambiguity. Let's begin by considering the role of the Bible in this process.

The Bible Does Not Speak Directly to All Problems.
The fact that the Bible doesn't speak to every problem you face may surprise you. Perhaps you've heard, "The Bible is God's eternal Word that comprehensively addresses every issue of life," or something to that effect. Certainly, the Bible is God's eternal Word. But does it address *every* issue of life in a comprehensive way?

Surely not. The Bible doesn't talk about single parents or whether you should work in a bomb factory. It doesn't address the nuances of bankruptcy. It doesn't deal with the complex issues surrounding AIDS or the international implications of thermonuclear war. It doesn't say what age is best for retirement, or give instructions on how to fire someone or how much health insurance or worker's compensation an employer should provide. It doesn't address the host of issues surrounding women in today's workplace, or the question of how moral responsibility should be assessed in a corporation.

There are scores of issues like these that you and I face every day that the Bible doesn't address *directly*. So we have to be careful when we say things like, "The Bible has the answers for every problem we might face." We may be assigning to Scripture a role that God never intended it to play.

Some Christians want to use the Bible like a computer: just feed in your moral questions, and out will come the authorized answer for right and wrong. In my experience, people who want that tend toward a rigid, legalistic, moralistic way of living. They can't make a move without biblical authorization. Is that what God intended?

I think a more helpful metaphor for using the Bible is suggested by David in Psalm 119:105: "Thy word is a lamp to my feet, and a light to my path." Picture yourself as being on a journey over a treacherous mountain path in the middle of the night with a driving rainstorm making things slippery and confusing your sense of direction. What do you need more than anything else? A light, so that you can see to stay on the path!

The Bible is our light in the midst of moral darkness. What does a light do? Does it make up your mind for you? Does it even tell you which way to go? No, it reveals the path; it shows you the way things are, so that you can make wise choices about your progress.

Now that's what the Bible does: It shows us the way things are—about ourselves, life, God, the world now, the world to come, and so on. It tells us everything we need to know to make intelligent, wise, ethically-sound decisions— decisions that honor God.

The Bible is a powerful and timeless book! It doesn't matter that its original context was rooted in cultures vastly different from our own. The fundamental dynamics of how to make moral choices are the same today as they were 2,000 or 3,000 years ago. Obviously, we often need to "culturally translate" the Bible's teaching into our modern day, but the underlying principles remain the same.

Perhaps it would help to point out the four levels on which the Bible can relate to issues that you face. The first level is *prohibitions*: instructions that are clear and straightforward, apply directly and unequivocally to specific areas of life, and are stated mostly in the negative, in terms of what you must not do. "You shall not murder" (Exodus 20:13) is an example of a biblical prohibition.

A second level has to do with the Bible's *positive commands*. These are easy to understand and speak to broad, general areas of behavior. Applying them to a specific situation may take some thought and creativity. "Walk in love" (Ephesians 5:2) is a positive command. So is "Husbands, love your wives, just as Christ also loved the church" (Ephesians 5:25).

A third level of biblical instruction is *values and principles*. I'll say much more about these in a moment.

The fourth level is the area of *conscience*. Matters of conscience occur when there are no clear prohibitions of Scripture that apply unequivocally to a situation. Instead, you have to forge a response out of whatever positive commands and principles you believe apply. In this area God leaves you with a great deal of latitude in what you decide to do. We'll consider several matters of conscience later in this chapter.

Applying these four levels of biblical instruction to life is what the Bible calls *wisdom*, which literally means "the skill of living." We particularly need wisdom as we consider the last two levels—principles and matters of conscience. Here are three keys to developing wisdom: regularly apply the Word to every area of life; learn from past experiences, both successes and failures; and spend time with others who exhibit biblical wisdom. Proverbs 2:1-5 promises that such wisdom comes to those who really *want* it:

> My son, if you will receive my sayings,
> And treasure my commandments within you,
> Make your ear attentive to wisdom,
> Incline your heart to understanding;
> For if you cry for discernment,
> Lift your voice for understanding;
> If you seek her as silver,
> And search for her as for hidden treasures;
> Then you will discern the fear of the LORD,
> And discover the knowledge of God.

Know the Bible and Commit Yourself to Obeying It.

It almost seems superfluous to mention that we must know the Bible and obey what is clearly taught. Yet I find that many who complain that the Bible is of no help turn out to be ignorant of what it actually says. By not reading it regularly and weaving it into their thinking, they're losing out on the vast resources of Scripture that God has provided, "making wise the simple" (Psalm 19:7).

Look for Principles in Scripture, Not Just Commands.

No doubt you've heard the familiar proverb: "Give a man a fish and you feed him for a day; teach a man to fish and you feed him for a lifetime." A similar idea comes into play as we read the Bible. God could have given us an encyclopedia of do's and don'ts that would have covered every possible detail of our moral lives. (It would have been akin to the Old Testament Law, only volumes longer!) But instead of that, He gave us something much more powerful: an extensive treasure house of truths and principles about life communicated in narrative, history, poetry, apocalyptic, didactic, and other forms of divinely inspired literature. He also gave us the human capacity to read His Word with skill, glean from its wisdom, and apply its truth to our lives.

This gives us a tremendously powerful and flexible tool that can be used anywhere, anytime. The key to this arrangement is the idea of *principles.* Principles are basic truths taught by the Bible that apply to life. The truth may be explicitly taught or merely implied by the overall context. So when you read any passage of Scripture, look not only for the immediate meaning of the text, but for the underlying principles as well.

For instance, in 1 Timothy 3:3, Paul lists the qualifications for elders: "Not addicted to wine or pugnacious, but gentle, uncontentious, free from the love of money." The phrase "free from the love of money," in context, clearly states that the elders, who are responsible for spiritual oversight, must not have a reputation for greed. Money must not entwine itself around their affections so that it rules them. That's obvious from the passage.

But isn't there an underlying principle? Isn't the passage implying something about money and greed that applies to all of us? If freedom from the love of money should characterize our spiritual leaders, shouldn't it be something that we all pursue?

In this manner, we arrive at principles to use in making moral choices. Even when we can't find an issue addressed directly in the Bible, we can always find basic principles that speak to the heart of our situation. (You might review my discussion of bankruptcy in chapter 10 as an example of how I use principles to determine how to handle a subject not directly addressed in Scripture.)

As you look for underlying principles in Scripture, keep in mind that to be valid, principles must have clear support from the entire Bible. You can't read into the text to make it say something it doesn't say. Likewise, avoid wrenching any verse out of its immediate context. I recall a rather tragic instance of this by a man accused of beating children. As a part of his twisted logic, he justified the injuries he inflicted by saying, "I'm just following God's will. Remember, Jesus said, 'Suffer the little children.' He wants them to suffer so that they'll learn to love Him." Need I say more?!

Context is so important—the local context of surrounding verses and the overall context of the Bible as a whole. Whatever principles you find need to be consistent with the rest of Scripture to be valid. If you come up with something that contradicts the clear teaching of the Bible, you are wide of the mark.

Furthermore, valid principles are those that have a practical application to life. What would a person do or not do if he lived by the principle you have found? If you can't say for sure, then you need to study Scripture more carefully. Remember, God wants His truth to make a difference in our lives—not fill our heads with religious facts.

Use Biblical Principles to Determine How You Should Respond to Moral Ambiguity.

When you're faced with a situation that doesn't seem to be addressed specifically in Scripture, you have a measure of freedom to decide how you should respond. I say "a measure" of freedom because you must never respond in a way that violates the express teaching of the Bible. For example, if you work for a company that has a bad record of polluting the environment, you won't find any verses that tell you whether or not to quit. So you have freedom to choose. But you don't have freedom to undercut management's authority, according to 1 Peter 2:13-18.

You must apply biblical principles to the gray areas you face. Start by defining your problem. What is it about the situation that is morally objectionable or questionable? Is it a case of deception or illegality? What standards and values are you being asked to compromise? In short, what is the fundamental issue at stake?

In the case of working for a polluter, I see the fundamental issue as one of integrity in the area of stewardship of the creation God has given us. Specifically, the question is this: Is it right to participate in an organization that carelessly and thoughtlessly spoils the environment?

Having nailed down the fundamental issue(s) in your situation, you're now ready to go to Scripture to find fundamental principles that might apply to those issues. In the example, I suggest a thorough review of passages that speak of God's concern for the earth and the responsibility He has delegated to man to care for it (i.e., Genesis 1-2 and Psalms 8, 104). In such passages you'll find principles regarding the relationship between man and the environment that will give you helpful insight into the course of action you should take. These are by no means the only issues you must consider; there are many specific factors about your situation that you'll have to weigh as well.

As you seek God's wisdom and use it to reflect on your situation, you'll come to a conclusion that has integrity before the Lord. It may not be what someone else would do, but you have freedom to apply God's Word as best you can to your situation. God will honor you for seeking His will. Psalm 19:9-11 promises,

The fear of the LORD is clean, enduring forever;
The judgments of the LORD are true; they are righteous
    altogether.
They are more desirable than gold, yes, than much
    fine gold;
Sweeter also than honey and the drippings of the
    honeycomb.

Listen to Your Conscience.

I'm amazed at how often people will violate their con-
sciences and do what they feel is wrong, even if they can't
explain why they feel that way. The conscience is a God-
given faculty for detecting right and wrong, particularly in
cases of moral ambiguity. A morally mature person is one
whose conscience is healthy and well-developed, having
fed itself on the Word of God (Hebrews 5:14): "Solid food is
for the mature, who because of practice have their senses
trained to discern good and evil."

Think of your conscience as a sense, such as the sense
of smell. Smell is able to detect odors, even though they are
invisible. Having detected them, you are then able to
deduce their source. In dealing with issues of integrity, you
need to cultivate a nose for right and wrong. Situations that
are ambiguous at first usually end up crystal clear in the end.
Your conscience can help you detect early on which way
things are headed.

Learn to Distinguish Between Direct
and Indirect Participation in Evil.

I'm frequently given a scenario that goes something like
this: "Doug, I work for an employer in such-and-such
an industry. And this employer is doing such-and-such
wrong. Should I be working for this company? Am I guilty
of being an accomplice in this wrongdoing, even though

I'm not directly involved in it?"

I suspect you can find a situation like this in your own job. Perhaps you're an employer whose company employs people who take drugs, commit adultery, cheat on their taxes, and so forth. Are you helping them underwrite such immorality by employing them? Maybe your product is something like airplane glue that kids use to get high. Are you guilty of complicity by manufacturing such a product? It could be that you work in a prison where life is unspeakably raw. You're told to take action on only the worst offenses, and let the rest go. As a result, you see numerous violations and injustices. Are you guilty because you fail to act?

I think the key to resolving questions like these is to distinguish between direct and indirect participation in evil. Direct participation involves a conscious, willful agreement to do what you know is wrong. If I rob a bank, I'm directly participating in evil. If I lie to a customer, steal a computer program, go to bed with my coworker, or get roaring drunk at an office party, I'm directly participating in evil. I stand guilty before God as having violated His clear, unequivocal commands.

In the cases mentioned earlier, the employer is not in business to subsidize immorality; he doesn't do so by design. The glue manufacturer makes glue for constructive purposes; he cannot be responsible for the misuse of his product. The prison guard is trying to maintain some modicum of order in an unusually violent, dangerous situation; he's not promoting wrongdoing, even though he sees it all the time.

In situations like these, the involvement with evil is there, but it's only indirect. It's an involvement that is not willfully promoting evil, even though it indirectly enables it. I believe that God does not hold a person guilty for such indirect participation in evil.

As you evaluate situations that trouble your conscience, ask yourself whether or not you are actively engaging in something that's wrong. If not, if you're involved only at a distance—several steps removed from the action—then you're probably not responsible for the evil taking place. That doesn't mean you should close your eyes to it and go about your business. You may still have good reason to take action. But don't place yourself under false guilt for the sinful actions of others.

If Everyone Else Is Doing It, Watch Out!
Too many of us let the crowd determine the ethics of what we do. Romans 12:2 calls this "conformity to the world," and warns us against it:

> And do not be conformed to this world, but be transformed by the renewing of your mind, that you may prove what the will of God is, that which is good and acceptable and perfect.

J.B. Phillips paraphrases this beautifully: "Don't let the world around you squeeze you into its own mold." Usually we think of this "bad influence" in terms of direct solicitations to evil: sexual temptation, greed, ridicule of biblical truth. But the really subtle and powerful influence comes in the gray areas, where no one is able to clearly say what is right and what is wrong.

In ambiguous situations, it's a good bet that the crowd will generally stick together—and be wrong. After all, think back to our discussion of how familiarity with Scripture acts like a moral compass to guide us through the fog. How could people who do not know God's Word and who do not want to please Him point toward a way that pleases Him? More likely, nonbelievers would be led by various influences of the flesh, the world, and the devil.

So in matters of moral ambiguity, if everyone at work seems to head together in a general direction, don't automatically start running with the pack. Sure, they all claim to be "doing their own thing," but it's remarkable how often that ends up as doing the same thing—the wrong thing. You should be the one marching to a different drumbeat (Ephesians 4:17-20):

> This I say therefore, and affirm together with the Lord, that you walk no longer just as the Gentiles also walk, in the futility of their mind, being darkened in their understanding, excluded from the life of God, because of the ignorance that is in them, because of the hardness of their heart; and they, having become callous, have given themselves over to sensuality, for the practice of every kind of impurity with greediness. But you did not learn Christ in this way.

Learn to Tolerate Moral Ambiguity.

By now it should be obvious that you're always going to face situations where there doesn't seem to be any clear indication of right or wrong, and where the best course of action is hard to discern. We might prefer a world with infinitely clearer blacks and whites, but we're not going to have it, not now anyway. Instead, we're stuck with ninety-nine shades of gray. Yet I think this is by God's design.

In a world of moral ambiguity, we have a distinctive opportunity to see who really loves God, who has a passion for pleasing Him. In fact, I believe moral ambiguity causes us to seek Him more than we would in a clearly defined situation. When the way is unclear, it's not too hard to spot those who are serious about integrity; they're the ones sifting through the Scriptures, praying at every step, carefully and purposely making choices on the basis of their best estimate of God's will. In short, they're the ones who "hunger and thirst for righteousness" (Matthew 5:6). "They shall be satisfied" by integrity!

How different this is from the person who drifts through life like a stick in a brook, swept along by the currents of popular opinion, following the path of least resistance. He's very much like the young fool in Proverbs 7, wandering around in a dangerous part of town. Sooner or later, his moral immaturity will lead him into ruin. That's not the outcome you want!

You want to preserve your integrity, not try to see how much wrongdoing you can get away with. By saturating your mind with Scripture and applying biblical principles to the situations you face, you'll go far in the direction of godliness. This is the promise of biblical wisdom (Proverbs 8:17): "I love those who love me; and those who diligently seek me will find me."

FOUR CASE STUDIES

Here is a chance to apply the principles we've considered through four situations that involve moral ambiguity. These are four actual scenarios to which I've been asked to respond. See what you make of them. (You may want to refer back to the eight strategic principles I've presented.)

Is It Right to Work in a Store that Sells Pornography?

A young man told me that he worked behind the checkout counter of a convenience store. The chain that owned the store placed soft-core pornographic magazines on a rack at the counter. He wondered whether it was right for him to be ringing up sales of such material. Should he find another job? Or should he just ignore it?

Is It Right to Work Where Alcohol Is Sold to Derelicts?
A man contacted me and said he'd been out of work for several months. Previously, he had quit his job as the manager of a pharmacy. In his state, pharmacies are allowed to sell alcohol. The store he'd managed happened to be in a part of town where homeless alcoholics were numerous. They would stand or lie outside his store in the morning, waiting for it to open so they could buy cheap booze.

Later, he'd see them sprawled on the street, in the alleys, and in the parks, passed out from the liquor he sold. He was so troubled by this that after much prayer and soul-searching, he had quit to look for another job.

Months went by, and no job offers came. Finally, as his family was running out of money, his old company called him and asked if he would return to his job as a pharmacy manager. If he asked you what you thought he should do, what would you tell him?

Is It Right to Sell Luxury Items?
Once I was speaking on the dignity of work and the implications of a biblical view of work for the kinds of jobs we do. My point was that we should use our God-given skills and abilities to make the greatest contribution we can to people.

I was then asked by a real estate broker whether it was the best use of his skills to be handling prestigious real estate for well-heeled clients. Wouldn't God rather have him working in a full-time Christian ministry somewhere?

This led into the broader question of working with luxury items in general. Is this legitimate before God? If so, why? If not, why not?

Is It Right to Be Involved in the Cigarette Industry?
I am often asked whether there are occupations that a Christian ought never to be involved in In response, I

always distinguish between legitimate and illegitimate kinds of work. Legitimate work is work that serves the legitimate needs of people. Illegitimate work is obviously work that does not serve people, or that actually harms them.

In your opinion, is work that involves the manufacture, distribution, or marketing of cigarettes something that Christians should be involved in? How do you see this issue?

CHAPTER TWELVE

Count Me Out

*Don't let peer pressure squeeze you into a
mold of conformity and compromise.*

D o you remember a little book called *Jonathan Livingston Seagull*? It's hard to find anyone today who will
admit to having read it, but in its day it was a best-selling
blockbuster. The story (so I'm told) is about a sea gull,
Jonathan, who dreams of flying with a grace and beauty
unequaled by his fellow sea gulls. So vivid and powerful is
his imagination that he actually succeeds in his quest for
perfection. But he does so only by resisting and ignoring the
flock of gulls who berate him and say it can't be done.

The story is a sort of "ugly duckling," sixties-style. It's
the age-old tale of an unlikely protagonist surmounting the
odds and the nay-saying of his peers to do the near-
impossible. It's the narrative of Don Quixote, Abraham
Lincoln, the Wright brothers, Horatio Alger, or Sam Walton.
It's the classic notion of doing what everyone swore could
not be done.

When it comes to maintaining your integrity, you may
feel like a Jonathan Livingston Seagull. You may feel like
your peers deride your humble efforts to do what is right.
Indeed, you may take real abuse because of your Christian

convictions and values. It seems that the tide of opinion is usually against you if you're determined to honor God. As a result, too many of us are compromising ourselves. Too many of us are bowing to peer pressure and letting the crowd determine our values and responses. We're keeping the lid on our relationship with God, and go to work each day like spiritual undercover agents whose true identities must be protected at all costs. We're morally camouflaged, so that we look just like everyone else; there's little if any distinction between us and our nonChristian counterparts in matters of ethics.

It's natural to want to belong, to be a part of the gang. No one wants to feel left out. Nor should we be so obnoxious or so strange that we invite ostracism. But the urge to belong has to take a back seat when it comes to our integrity. No price is too great to pay to do what is right before God, even if that price is the displeasure or disapproval of our peers.

I think you can see some inherent dangers in being held hostage to what other people think. In the first place, it's terribly unhealthy for your emotional life. Are you so dependent on the approval of others that you deny your true feelings and check your normal responses? Do you strive so hard to please others that you let them set the agenda for your life?

Even more dangerous than the psychological damage is the spiritual damage you receive when you fear the opinions of others. Over and over again, the Scriptures warn us that our ultimate allegiance must be to God, not men. He's the One we need to please, not our peers. Consider just a few of these passages from Scripture. Proverbs 29:25 says, "The fear of man brings a snare, but he who trusts in the LORD will be exalted." Isaiah 2:22 cautions us: "Stop regarding man, whose breath of life is in his nostrils; for why should he be esteemed?" And in Galatians 1:10, Paul declared that caring about the approval of others would undercut the work God had for him:

> For am I now seeking the favor of men, or of God?
> Or am I striving to please men? If I were still trying to
> please men, I would not be a bond-servant of Christ.

In Matthew 23, Jesus pronounced His famous "woes" on the scribes and Pharisees—the hypocritical religious leaders of His day. Among their misdeeds He included a preference for positive review by the people (23:5-7):

> "But they do all their deeds to be noticed by men; for
> they broaden their phylacteries, and lengthen the
> tassels of their garments. And they love the place
> of honor at banquets, and the chief seats in the
> synagogues, and respectful greetings in the market
> places, and being called by men, Rabbi."

Such concern with pleasing men rather than God was not limited to the religious leaders, however. Jesus also told the crowds who followed Him that they were missing God's favor because they preferred the favor of each other instead of His (John 5:44): "How can you believe, when you receive glory from one another, and you do not seek the glory that is from the one and only God?"

In contrast to these cautions against worrying about peer pressure, we find scores of verses that encourage us to fear God instead. Deuteronomy 6:4-9 states it as an all-encompassing, overwhelming love for God that should be our highest concern. In this lengthy quote, notice the extreme emphasis on making the fear of the Lord prominent in one's everyday experience:

"Hear, O Israel! The LORD is our God, the LORD is one!
"And you shall love the LORD your God with all your heart and with all your soul and with all your might. And these words, which I am commanding you today, shall be on your heart; and you shall teach them diligently to your sons and shall talk of them when you sit in your house and when you walk by the way and when you lie down and when you rise up. And you shall bind them as a sign on your hand and they shall be as frontals on your forehead. And you shall write them on the doorposts of your house and on your gates."

Stressing its importance, the command is repeated later in Deuteronomy 10:12-13:

"And now, Israel, what does the LORD your God require from you, but to fear the LORD your God, to walk in all His ways and love Him, and to serve the LORD your God with all your heart and with all your soul, and to keep the LORD's commandments and His statutes which I am commanding you today for your good?"

This duty to concern ourselves chiefly with what God thinks is not limited to Israel (Psalm 33:8): "Let all the earth fear the LORD; let all the inhabitants of the world stand in awe of Him." And in Proverbs 3:7, Solomon challenges us to forsake our own popularity and to seek God's approval instead: "Do not be wise in your own eyes; fear the LORD and turn away from evil."

In 1 Peter 1, God's holiness and Christ's sacrifice on our behalf demand a response of holy fear and awe toward the Lord (1:17-19):

And if you address as Father the One who impartially judges according to each man's work, conduct yourselves in fear during the time of your stay upon earth; knowing that you were not redeemed with perishable things like silver or gold from your futile way of life inherited from your forefathers, but with precious blood, as of a lamb unblemished and spotless, the blood of Christ.

If we are too concerned with what people think, we'll live in bondage to them. We'll be wretched as we seek to please them and prompt their approval. But when our main purpose is to serve God and please Him, we enjoy numerous benefits. We receive honor from God (Psalm 15:4). We enjoy intimacy with God (Psalm 25:14, 66:16-20). We feel His love and concern (Psalm 33:18, 147:11) as well as His protection (Psalm 34:7, 60:4-5, 85:9; Proverbs 14:26). We find that He meets our needs (Psalm 34:9-10, 111:5). We learn true wisdom (Psalm 111:10; Proverbs 1:7, 9:10, 15:33). We enjoy prolonged life (Proverbs 10:27, 14:27, 19:23). We also avoid evil (Proverbs 16:6). Many more benefits could be mentioned, but it's obvious that we can only lose by striving to please people rather than God. Not only do their opinions count for very little, but following them will bring us only grief if they are opposed to God. By contrast, we enjoy things that others will never experience when our aim is to love and serve Jesus Christ.

Of course, there's actually a benefit to others when we stand up and stand out for God. We become a light to them, showing the way toward Christ. Jesus said that this is part of our purpose in living (Matthew 5:10-16):

"Blessed are those who have been persecuted for the sake of righteousness, for theirs is the kingdom of heaven. Blessed are you when men cast insults at you, and persecute you, and say all kinds of evil against you falsely, on account of Me. Rejoice, and be glad, for your reward in heaven is great, for so they persecuted the prophets who were before you.

"You are the salt of the earth; but if the salt has become tasteless, how will it be made salty again? It is good for nothing anymore, except to be thrown out and trampled under foot by men.

"You are the light of the world. A city set on a hill cannot be hidden. Nor do men light a lamp, and put it under the peck-measure, but on the lampstand; and gives light to all who are in the house. Let your light shine before men in such a way that they may see your good works, and glorify your Father who is in heaven."

Notice the context. Jesus starts by saying that persecution is preferable to praise, because it probably means you are doing what is right. Persecution, slander, threats, ostracism—these are a good indication that you are living distinctively for God (see Luke 6:26). Like salt, you are to penetrate the culture with a Christlike influence. If you're not having any influence, then you have become tasteless, morally washed out, and essentially washed up as far as any testimony is concerned.

Then Jesus likens us to a beacon of light, placed strategically where all can see it. You are placed in your workplace to light the way to Christ for your coworkers. That's by no means the only reason you're there, but it's certainly an important one.

Are you shining forth in a way that pleases God and influences others? Or have you covered up your light through moral camouflage and compromise? Jesus urges you that your lifestyle and workstyle should be so unique and distinctive that coworkers would want to know why. Paul repeats this theme in Philippians 2:14-15 (NIV):

> Do everything without complaining or arguing, so that you may become blameless and pure, children of God without fault in a crooked and depraved generation, in which you shine like stars in the universe.

After you read through the various statistics presented in chapter 2, did you have any doubt that we live and work in the midst of "a crooked and depraved generation"? I'm not demeaning the inherent worth and dignity of the people we work with. But from a moral point of view, and especially from God's perspective, people do twisted and corrupt things. They are victims, in many ways, of the condition that the Bible calls sin. Worst of all, they are utterly lost in moral darkness.

Are you shining like a star in that darkness? If you were the only point of light by which your coworkers could navigate toward the refuge of God, would there be enough brightness to guide them? It can't happen if you extinguish yourself out of fear of rejection or disapproval.

Instead of letting others set the pace for you, why not become a pacesetter yourself—a leader for Christlike thinking and influence in your workplace? Proverbs 12:26 affirms, "The righteous is a guide to his neighbor." In the next chapter we'll look at how you can guide others toward the light of Christ.

CHAPTER THIRTEEN

Shine Like a Star
You can be a leader for moral and ethical influence where you work.

Probably no question has received more attention in the last twenty years among church leaders and officials of mission organizations than, "How can we reach the world with the message of the gospel?"

How would you answer that if the task were up to you? Would you try to beef up missionary recruiting strategies so as to find the best people to send overseas? Would you raise and spend millions, as some have done, on media blitzes, publishing, and radio and television? Would you try for an increase in the more traditional approach of mass evangelistic crusades?

I think all of these strategies and more should be done. But my own belief is that *the workplace has become the most strategic arena for Christian thinking and influence today.* Whatever efforts are made, we should pay a lot more attention to the fact that nearly everyone works, that work is coming more and more to define the way life is lived, and that for many if not most nonChristians, the workplace is the only place where they'll have a chance to see Christians— and therefore Christianity—up close.

165

Let me go a step further and say that whatever efforts ministries and missions exert through their programs will have little effect if people don't see genuine Christianity at work. All the sermons, television shows, pamphlets, and crusades in the world are unlikely to overcome the deep skepticism people feel once they see a person who claims to know Christ compromise his integrity—especially if he does so repeatedly and unashamedly.

What this boils down to, then, is *your* integrity before a watching world. In the last chapter, I cautioned against bowing to the pressures around you to conform to ungodly standards and behaviors. The flip side is that your lifestyle, if it remains Christlike, can have a profound effect on others. Recall Philippians 2:14-15 (NIV):

> Do everything without complaining or arguing, so that you may become blameless and pure, children of God without fault in a crooked and depraved generation, in which you shine like stars in the universe.

God has placed you in the midst of moral darkness to light the way toward Him. As you shine like a star where you work, you can influence your coworkers toward Christ. If the workplace is the most strategic arena for Christian thinking and influence today, it's because *you are the most strategic figure in the cause of Christ today.* You can have a profound impact for Christ where you work, on at least two levels.

YOUR INFLUENCE ON COWORKERS

Have you ever considered how strategically placed you are? "Oh sure!" I hear someone saying. "I'm a plumber. I'm an aircraft technician. I work on an assembly line with hundreds of other people. I don't have any power or any say over what goes on. I'm no Bible scholar. And I'm certainly no Billy Graham!" My response to that is: That's why you're so strategic!

Suppose you and I decided that we wanted to hold a week-long evangelistic crusade in your city. We'd have to start months ahead of time to plan it, to line up our helpers, and to raise the money. After considerable effort and expense by scores of people, we might be able to attract a total attendance of 5,000, maybe as many as 10,000 or 20,000 if we had a well-known evangelist speak. That would be a one-time event. And we'd hope that we would see a few hundred people come to faith in Christ.

Now by contrast, think about your workplace. Every day your employer brings together dozens if not hundreds of workers. He pays for the building, and he gives you eight hours a day to be with them—day after day. Furthermore, there are quite likely others around you who also have a relationship with Christ. Collectively, you have an impressive opportunity for influence.

The Communists figured this out long ago. Douglas Hyde, a former party boss, explains why the Communists have found the workplace to be such a productive recruiting ground:

> The most important part of the Communist's day is, or should be, that which he spends at work. He sees his work as giving him a wonderful opportunity to do a job for the cause. By way of contrast, the average [Christian] feels that his time for going into action on behalf of his beliefs begins after he has returned from his day's work, had a meal, changed and has just an hour or two left—when he is already tired—to give to his cause.[1]

I think Hyde is extremely perceptive. His observations are right on target. Communism may be collapsing today under the weight of its own internal contradictions, but its workplace strategy to get its message out in noncommunist countries is still as strong as ever. I submit that in North America we are seeing the same dynamics at work in the ideology known as secularism. Different worldview, same strategy: Showcase your ideas and activities where people work, and you'll not only gain a hearing, you'll win converts.

How long will it be before Christians wake up to this reality? Most of us think of "ministry" and religious activity as something we do on our own time. Activities like Bible studies, volunteer projects, prayer meetings, softball games, pool parties, concerts—these are where we put our time and energy on behalf of our "Christian life." But like a set of golf clubs or the lawn mower, we put our religion away when it's time to go back to work, to the "real world."

I think you, at least, can do better! I believe you can have a far more strategic impact for Christ where you work. Your faith can be much more relevant in your day-to-day affairs, and therefore relevant to your coworkers, who fundamentally have the same interests as you, the same concerns, the same problems to solve. What they don't have is Christ. You do.

You can exhibit leadership in your workplace by how you work, by how you live, and by what you say. In that order! Let's consider these in detail.

Exhibit Leadership By How You Work.
In his excellent book *Dedication and Leadership*, Hyde includes a chapter on work entitled, "You Must Be the Best." I can't urge you strongly enough to obtain Hyde's book and read that chapter. If you do, you'll never regard

your work in the same way.

Hyde points out that the people who command the greatest respect in the workplace are the ones who do the best work. We see this all the time. The top salespeople, the most proficient surgeons, the sharpest lawyers, the strongest hard hats, the winningest athletes—they may be a real cuss to get along with, but one thing's for certain: when they talk, people listen, not only when they speak in their area of expertise, but even when they speak about politics, philosophy, religion, art, or even an area they know very little about! Sure it's crazy. As Hyde says,

> It may be quite irrational, but the fact is that, if you are recognized as being outstanding at work, you will be listened to on all sorts of subjects in no way related to it.[2]

Consequently, he says, "if you are going to be really effective [in having an influence] in your place of work, you must set out to be the best man at your job."

If you're a deadbeat at work, if you show up late and leave early, pass responsibilities on to others, trample coworkers' rights, abuse customers, gripe about the boss to others, gripe about others to the boss, ignore personal hygiene and grooming, dress like a slob, and change jobs too frequently, nobody will listen to you about *anything*, least of all the gospel! They just won't take you seriously.

I believe that the place to start, if you want to advance the cause of Christ at your workplace, is to be the best worker you can possibly be. Forget trying to learn an evangelistic spiel or steer conversations toward Christ *until* you are a good worker. The biblical precedent for this approach is in Titus 2:9-10 (NIV), a passage we encountered before in connection with obeying authority:

Teach slaves to be subject to their masters in everything, to try to please them, not to talk back to them,
and not to steal from them, but to show that they can
be fully trusted, so that in every way they will make
the teaching about God our Savior attractive.

Notice again the practical ways suggested to make the
gospel attractive at work. Let me add further specifics: Treat
people with respect and courtesy, even if they are con-
temptible and rude. When conflicts and problems arise,
don't make mountains out of molehills; seek to preserve
relationships, and enlist others to work with you at solving
problems. Pray specifically for your boss, your associates,
and any workers under your authority, every day if you can.
Get organized, at least in a way that helps you get your work
done and helps your work fit in with the work of others. Put
in the hours that the job really demands and for which
you're getting paid. Seek jobs that make the very best use of
your God-given skills, abilities, and motivations. Improve
yourself and your skills by continually learning and accepting new opportunities. Celebrate others' victories and
breakthroughs like new contracts, the achievement of goals,
or the completion of a project, and *affirm* others.

I could easily fill a book with behaviors like these that
are part of an excellent work ethic, but I think you get the
point. No doubt you could devise a list of your own. I
encourage you to do so. What does excellence look like
where you work? Are you pursuing it? If not, you'll have a
difficult time influencing others to consider the claims of
Christ.

Exhibit Leadership By How You Live.
How you work is what I call your "workstyle." The quality of
life is your lifestyle. Does yours reflect Christlikeness? This

is an issue of character, and at the heart of your character should be integrity. People watch you all day long to see what you're really made of underneath the persona you project. They want to get past the image to the real you. What do they see when they look at you?

My prayer is that they would see someone *alive* inside! Someone who takes life seriously, but who doesn't take himself too seriously. Someone who is able to keep the urgency of immediate tasks in perspective with the larger, more important issues and values of life—and in turn, to keep those in perspective with eternity. Someone whose ethics can't be bought, whose integrity is beyond question. Someone who expresses compassion for others, and helps as he can. Someone who is desirable to have around. In short, someone who commands respect by the quality of his character, the sort of person whom others regard as a truly good human being.

Can you appreciate the power of that sort of lifestyle? It doesn't win through intimidation or overwhelm through manipulation; it appeals through genuine concern, humility, and authenticity. It's morally clean, but it's winsome and attractive, not self-righteous or judgmental. It's the sort of character that Christ produces in you when He's in control of your life.

Whether you realize it or not, your coworkers can tell whether He really is your Lord or whether religion is just something you talk about but doesn't make a difference in your life. They can hear it in your voice, see it in your eyes. They can tell by the way you talk with your spouse on the phone, how you greet people in the morning, how you drive your car, how you spend your money.

Your faith, you see, is not something that you communicate merely by talking about it. If it were, it would be nothing but a story. But it's a way of life that you cannot really escape. If Jesus is your Lord, it will be evident in how you live, and you'll surely gain a hearing for the gospel, even if you're unaware of it. If He's not your Lord, it's best not to say anything.

Exhibit Leadership By What You Say.

There will come a time, of course, when you should talk about Jesus. Maybe you'll initiate it, maybe others will ask you. But sooner or later, if your life and work warrant it, it will be appropriate to explain what lies behind everything you do and are.

It's impossible to predict exactly what you need to say in that moment, or how you need to say it. That's largely a function of your personality, as well as the context of the conversation. Whatever you do, be honest and clear. I personally believe that every Christian needs to memorize a concise explanation of the gospel. I say "memorize" and I mean it; you should be able to wake up out of a dead sleep and spit it out. That way, you won't forget it when it comes time to tell someone how she can enter into a relationship with Christ.

But not every conversation about spiritual things needs to end in a gospel presentation. I suggest that when talking about your faith you tell what you know—not just what you know in your head, but what you know by *experience*. Don't be afraid that your walk with Christ may not sound as dramatic, as fascinating, or as mystical as others'. Talk about what your walk with God means for you and what He has done for *you*. To the extent that you can, be ready to explain the biblical basis for your faith and experience.

If someone asks you something you don't know, by all means just say, "I don't know," and then offer to find out. I don't recommend spending a lot of time on hypothetical scenarios and theological speculations. Those usually lead nowhere because they come from nowhere. I wouldn't waste time seriously discussing matters that really make no difference to anyone.

I think you'll gain more interest if you allow others to tell you what they want to know. They will if you let them. For instance, if someone asks, "Why do you go to church?" he's likely asking for a *brief* explanation of the importance of religion in your life. After all, why go to church as opposed to any number of other things you could do on a Sunday? You could answer this query in about two sentences. Notice that he is *not* asking for a defense of your particular church over another, or for a complete rundown of all the programs and activities at your church along with their times and who leads them, or for a thorough catechism of what your church stands for, its history, and its future!

Simple question, simple answer. This goes hand in hand with a related principle of discussing spiritual things: Less is more. Some of us have heard so many sermons that we want to preach a few ourselves. So when somebody shows the *slightest* interest, the dam bursts and we tell them everything they never wanted to know about what we believe, why, and what it means for them. It's a poor strategy. Better to leave them longing, not loathing. You might try telling less than what you could. If the person is genuinely interested, he'll ask for more. That way, you allow him to keep the conversation going and to set its agenda.

So if asked why I go to church, I might respond, "My faith is important to me. It's a part of how I live and work. So I go to church to encourage it and make it stronger." Then I'd shut up. Just in those sentences I've given the person plenty to think about. He may want to leave it at that, or he may want to ask follow-up questions, but that decision should be his. I *certainly* wouldn't turn the tables on him with a question like, "How come you *don't* go to church?"

You may be wondering whether I'm somehow embarrassed about my walk with Christ that I wouldn't be more aggressive. By no means! The truth is, personally, I would probably tend to be more aggressive than what I'm describing. But I realize that not everyone is like that, so I don't want to make my style normative. Furthermore, I'm painfully aware that too many Christians have given the gospel a bad reputation by their crude, insensitive, soapbox approach to evangelism. What's worse, many do it without a lifestyle and workstyle to back it up.

The order is terribly important! If you want to win a hearing for the gospel, start by being the best worker you can be, and gain the respect of your peers. Match that workstyle with a lifestyle so unique and distinctive that your coworkers will want to know why. If that happens, you'll have plenty of opportunities to discuss your faith. And when you do, you'll find yourself having a powerful impact on others.

INFLUENCING YOUR ORGANIZATION

Before leaving this issue of your impact in the workplace, let me challenge you if you're in a position of formal leadership in your company. If you're a supervisor, manager, executive, CEO, owner, partner, trustee—in short, if you're a decision-maker at any level in your workplace—Christ should have a definite influence on you and your decisions, and through you on your organization.

Now let me be clear in what I am *not* saying. I do not believe that Christ wants Christians to take over corporations and turn them into Christian IBMs, or to elect only Christians into government and turn the country into a Christian nation. Some believers feel that this is what God wants, but I believe they are mistaken. That's a misinterpretation of God's Word and a misapplication of energy.

Such a scenario sounds appealing, but it misunderstands the way God works. If we as Christians were to take over the nation and start legislating morality and ethics, we would be trying to change people from the outside in. The strategy would be that the right rules render the right kind of people. But when we turn to Scripture we find that God changes people from the inside out. He transforms by the renewing of the mind (Romans 12:2) and the heart (Romans 6:17-18, 10:9-10).

It's not until people are right with God and have their fundamental condition of sin dealt with that they are even able to please God and obey Him (Romans 8:7, Ephesians 5:8). That's why it's so critical that we influence people toward Christ at the individual level. You doubtless see many things in your company and in your society that need change. Press for such change, but realize that your most effective impact will be on the person working next to you. If you're on an assembly line, ask God to allow you to win even one other person on the line for Him. If you're a manager, seek to share Christ with other managers. If you're a CEO, use your contacts with other CEOs to win a hearing for the gospel.

How, then, can you use your position in the organization to strategic ethical advantage? Recall that in chapter 2 I mentioned that some research strongly indicates that when it comes to ethics the tone is set from the top down. The higher you are in an organization, the greater your influence on the ethical climate under you. It's not something you have to try to have; it's something you already have.

How can you make the best of your situation? Let me point out that if you are the owner of the business, you have almost total control over the way business is to be conducted, and how employees are to behave. Depending on the size of your company, I don't think you'll be able to hire only Christians, and I'm not sure I'd recommend it. Whether all your executives are believers is up to you, but again, I'd look for quality workers and quality people over Christian antecedents.

However, I definitely suggest that you devise an ethics policy, or at least a code of conduct that spells out what the moral expectations are and how infractions will be handled. In putting this together, I would discuss with your people what kinds of ethical issues and dilemmas they frequently confront in the conduct of the business. Additional strategies for setting the tone include: executive training in ethical decision making; employee training along the same lines for issues at their level; screening of potential employees as far as their moral predisposition; and of course regular dialogue with people at all levels of your company to keep yourself informed of problems, successes, and developments in this area.

You can also encourage your people, especially executives, to promote justice and fairness throughout the organization. Reinforce and reward instances of honesty and integrity. Likewise, correct situations where employees have acted dishonestly. By applying broad principles of integrity to your organization—principles with which most people will agree—you'll avoid any sense of "forcing your religion" on others.

As for the question of company Bible studies, I would encourage them and let those who want to participate in them, but I would never make them mandatory, nor would I recommend that you be the one to lead them. In our book *Your Work Matters to God*, Bill and I discuss the value of small group discussion among workers and how to structure them. Of all the ways to promote life-change, I think small groups of peers discussing workplace issues from a biblical perspective are the most effective, and I heartily encourage you to consider starting this type of group.

What if you're not the owner of your company? Suppose you're one executive in a Fortune 500 conglomerate, or a sales manager for a medium-sized manufacturing concern. How can you promote integrity in your position? You have limited control over what happens, and your organization may formally or informally discourage any intrusion of religion into the workplace, so you have to be wise in how you extend influence. My suggestion is that, in the decision-making process, you use whatever voice you have and whatever power you wield to sway things in the direction of moral integrity.

Say a problem with an employee is brought to your attention: a supervisor is being unfair to one or two workers, and it's affecting morale. You have a chance to change that. When you pull the supervisor aside, I wouldn't suggest that you spout Bible verses. If the person's a nonChristian, he'll resent it and may even complain that you are trying to force your religion on him. Instead, I recommend that you appeal to him along the broader lines of justice, fair play, and employee morale. Obviously you need to get his side of the story, and consider the facts. But you are in a position to tell him what is acceptable and what isn't.

Another situation is when you're part of a joint decision with several others. If you sense that matters are heading in an unethical direction, speak up, but appeal to the others on the basis of general standards of right and wrong, on the basis of justice, on the basis of human dignity and value, or on the basis of the reputation of the company. You won't always persuade your colleagues. Sometimes you'll be out-voted, or your superiors may overturn your decision. But just by voicing your concerns and explaining why, you let others know that someone is evaluating decisions with an eye toward integrity. That alone may keep things clean, or at least keep them more clean than they would be.

In 1987, Beechnut was indicted on 215 felony counts in connection with the manufacture and sale of beet sugar water as apple juice for infants. The defendants were eventually found guilty on all counts and sentenced with prison terms and fines, though these were later overturned on appeal. The final outcome is still pending.

Suppose you were an executive at Beechnut, and you learned about this deception. Suppose you were at a meeting where this matter was discussed. Would you have been willing to speak up, to challenge the ethics involved, to risk the disapproval of others, and perhaps even vaporize your corporate career? Then again, would you have been willing to save Beechnut from public disgrace and censure, to save some of your peers—or yourself—the agony and expense of a court trial and the horror of conviction and possible time in jail, to say nothing of the ruin to their careers?

The situations at your company may or may not be as dramatic as at Beechnut, but every day you face choices where your commitment to Christ should play a role. Don't be fooled into thinking that you should somehow leave your religion and worldview at home and instead be philosophically neutral in your position of leadership. No one else lives that way, least of all those who advance that proposition. Moreover, no one *can* live that way. Everyone has some basis for his actions and choices, even if he's completely secular.

Whatever position of leadership you have is a responsibility and a resource given to you by God. Your ultimate allegiance must be to Him. As you exercise authority, use your influence to do the very best for your employer, but always wield it in a way that would please God. If and when those two conflict, you'll have to defer to God's will over your employer's. That may prove temporarily costly in your career, but it will result in eternal benefits that you won't want to forfeit, as we'll see in chapter 15. First, let's consider what you should do when you *don't* exercise moral leadership—when instead you sell your integrity and give way to compromise.

NOTES: 1. Douglas Hyde, *Dedication and Leadership* (Notre Dame, Ind.: University of Notre Dame Press, 1966), pages 97-98.
2. Hyde, page 98.

CHAPTER FOURTEEN

Picking Up the Pieces

What should you do when you've blown it?

H onesty. Obedience to authority. Resolving conflicts. Sexual purity. Trustworthiness. These are some of the wonderful ideals to which we as God's people aspire. Just as He is morally perfect and pure, so we long to cultivate unimpeachable integrity.

Yet the sad reality is that we'll never fully live up to our moral and ethical ideals. Because we are weakened by sin and rebellion against God by nature, we'll eventually blow it. Sooner or later we'll do the exact opposite of what we know to be right.

In fact, we're deluding ourselves if we think otherwise. Remember José Cubera, the bullfighter? I mentioned his name in connection with 1 Corinthians 10:12: "Therefore let him who thinks he stands take heed lest he fall." Recall how the bull that Cubera thought he had slain rallied, and fatally gored the unsuspecting hero. It's a gripping analogy to the fact that we're never beyond moral failure. If we ever think we are, that's a good sign that we're already on the way down!

Let me give you a for-instance, and use it as a case study

in discussing the matter of restoring our reputation and integrity once we've lost them.

When I was going through flight training as an Air Force pilot, I had an instructor that I couldn't stand! In fact, neither could any of my fellow students. He was vain. He was pugnacious. He was a real pain. Worst of all, he was a terrible instructor because he gave every instruction, every command, at the top of his voice. No matter what he said to us, he screamed! So we nicknamed him the Screamer.

One day I was assigned to fly in a plane under his direction. As the student, I sat in the front seat, and he sat behind me in the rear seat. The only way we could communicate was through our headsets.

It seemed like he screamed instructions at me from the time we went through our preflight briefing, through our checks, taxi, and takeoff, all the way out to the staging area. It wasn't a steady stream of screaming, but sudden outbursts. We'd be flying along smoothly and quietly, when suddenly—*bam*—my headset would explode with his shrill voice.

Worst of all, he seemed to anticipate by a nanosecond the very move I was about to execute. If I was getting ready to turn left, then just as I'd start to apply pressure on the stick to turn left, he'd scream, "Sherman, turn left!" It was so unnerving that sometimes I'd bungle the maneuver, and then he'd scream at me for bungling the maneuver! I couldn't win. After a while, I'd had enough of the Screamer. I felt like ejecting him into the big blue sky over the prairie!

As we were flying along, he suddenly screamed, "Sherman, dive!" I guess I didn't respond quickly enough, because the next thing I knew, my headset was jumping: "Sherman, I said dive! Do you know what dive means? When I say dive . . . ."

Okay, pal, I thought, *let's dive!* I slammed the stick forward as far as I could and executed a violent dive. In that type of supersonic aircraft, that move puts incredible stress on both the plane and the pilots. It also picks up all the dirt and debris from the floor and shoots it right up in the pilots' faces—but mostly in the face of the guy in back.

I about split a gut laughing inside as I heard the Screamer spluttering and wiping dirt from his eyes and face. Then he really started to scream at me, so I reached down and turned off my headset. The smooth, peaceful whoosh of the plane was now the only noise in my ears. I relaxed and felt quite satisfied, especially when I looked in my rear-view mirror and saw the instructor screaming his head off, red in the face, his arms waving frantically.

Since I pretty much knew the routine for our return to the base, I left the headset off until we pulled up to the hangar. Would you believe that after all of that, the instructor turned to me as we were heading back to the flight room and remarked, "That was a pretty good ride, Sherman. You handled the plane real well, just like I told you!"

I was dumbfounded! What's more, I began to feel very guilty. I knew that I had let my frustrations keep me from respecting this man's authority. And even though he felt fine about the ride and would have never known about my disrespect, I knew right then that I had acted poorly—and that I had to apologize. So I didn't put it off.

I followed my instructor into the flight room, waited until we were alone, and then approached him. "Sir, I need to make an apology," I began. He looked puzzled, as if to ask, "An apology for what?" So I continued: "I got upset by some things on the flight, so when you told me to make that dive, I did it in a way that would be unpleasant for you."

"Hey," he began to cut me short, "these things happen. I understand. Everybody gets a little tense when they're in training." He was trying to let me off the hook.

"But sir, you need to know that it wasn't okay for me to

lose my temper like that. You see, as a Christian that's not the way I'm supposed to deal with my anger. I'm sorry. I won't let it happen again."

Then it was his turn to be dumbfounded. In fact, he walked off, shaking his head. In the end we became fairly good friends, though I don't think he ever did understand why I apologized. But that didn't matter to me; I knew I had blown my cool, and blown my testimony as a follower of Christ. I could never have had peace about it until I apologized for my behavior. To this day, I'm not proud of what I did in that aircraft, even though it felt great at the time. But at least I salvaged my self-respect by doing what I could to set things right.

THE LONG ROAD BACK

Like me, you've probably blown it somewhere along the way. If you haven't already, just wait—you will! Sooner or later, each of us will fail in some area of integrity. Sometimes it's a private matter, like my episode with the flight instructor. Other times it's a public scandal that threatens to ruin the person's entire life. When you do fail, how can you recover? Suppose you're caught in a serious lie and dismissed from your job. Or you withhold important information from government inspectors and the omission is discovered later. Or an audit finds your personal expenses charged to company expense accounts. Or your supervisor catches you loafing in the break room during a busy period when you're supposed to be on the job. How will you recover?

In situations like these, our reputation is tarnished, sometimes irreparably. Furthermore, our witness as believers is compromised. Our self-respect is probably lost, or at least humiliated. And a cloud of guilt comes between us and

God. Is there a way out of this quagmire, a way to restore our reputation, dignity, intimacy with God, and integrity? Or if the offense is a serious one, are we somehow "put on the shelf" by God—forgiven, yes, but living the rest of our lives under a cloud of doubt as to our reliability?

I believe there is a way out and a way back. It's not an easy road to travel, and not everyone will travel it. Some people who fail become hardened in their rebellion, and slip deeper into compromise. But if you want to return to holiness, I can suggest a few steps you'll have to take.

Accept Your Undoing and Face the Truth Squarely.
The place to start heading back is to plead guilty and accept whatever that brings. If you are in the wrong, you can't deal with your sin unless you stop defending your innocence and admit, "I was wrong. I blew it."

Charles Colson slowly came to that point during the Watergate scandal. He had become a believer during the ordeal, and one of his first acts as a new Christian was to admit his complicity. For him that meant pleading guilty to obstruction of justice and doing time in prison for it. It was not a decision he arrived at easily, as he describes it in *Born Again* (Spire Books, 1977). But making it was the beginning of the end of his moral agony, the first step back on a long and painful road to recovery.

If you've fallen into ethical or moral compromise, and in your heart of hearts you know you're guilty, then you need to admit that, to yourself and to appropriate others.

Apologize to God and Anyone You've Wronged.
First John 1:9 is a verse often quoted by Christians: "If we confess our sins, He is faithful and righteous to forgive us our sins and to cleanse us from all unrighteousness." The spirit of this verse is not that we engage in some trivial ritual

of confession and then run off to repeat our sins. Rather, when we're finally ready to face our wrongs and deal with them, we need to start by admitting to God what we've done. We need to acknowledge our sins in every way we can, accepting responsibility for what we have done. I believe that if we are truly sorry for our failures, we'll usually feel a sense of grief and guilt that ought to be expressed as well.

The wonderful promise of 1 John 1:9 is that when we confess our sins, we find God ready to forgive, to set our lives right again, and to bring us back into close relation with Him. This is a tremendous expression of God's gracious love toward us. He wants the air cleared and us to enjoy communion with Him. But we must understand a delicate balance. On the one hand we need to recognize how freely God offers forgiveness. Yet this should never cause us to be casual about sin. In fact, our attitude toward evil should be hatred. In Proverbs we find that one measure of our fear of the Lord is our hatred of evil:

> The fear of the LORD is to hate evil;
> Pride and arrogance and the evil way,
> And the perverted mouth, I hate. (Proverbs 8:13)

So a part of our ethical edge is our hatred of evil. But the other aspect of this delicate balance is that once we have confessed our moral failure to God, we also must accept His forgiveness and forgive ourselves. There is something in our pride that finds it hard to accept forgiveness for our failures. We want to "pay our own way" for our sin. Accepting forgiveness when we know we don't *deserve* it is difficult.

Sometimes I get depressed over mistakes I have made. But biblically, God wants me to see myself as He does.

Wallowing in depression and not forgiving ourselves leaves us vulnerable to more sin. The Bible addresses two kinds of sorrow that come from sin. The first is a healthy response to guilt because we have failed, which leads to repentance and acceptance of God's forgiveness. A second form of sorrow comes when our pride is wounded, and we refuse to accept a right standing before God.

> For the sorrow that is according to the will of God produces a repentance without regret, leading to salvation; but the sorrow of the world produces death. (2 Corinthians 7:10)

A follower of Christ likely will ask for forgiveness several times a day—for everything from bad attitudes, to cursing another driver, to losing one's temper, and so on. The great thing about His forgiveness is that we don't have to say, "Well, Lord, I did it again." Because past sins have been forgiven.

> As far as the east is from the west, so far has He removed our transgressions from us. Just as the father has compassion on his children, so the LORD has compassion on those who fear Him. For He Himself knows our frame; He is mindful that we are but dust. (Psalm 103:12-14)

Apologizing to God for what you have done and accepting His forgiveness are both common and essential components of keeping your edge sharp. But it doesn't stop there. We should go to anyone else we have failed and acknowledge the same responsibility for what we've done to them. That's what I had to do with my flight instructor. It was a very hard thing to do! But apologizing to him was a helpful way to make sure I was really dealing with my sin (see James 5:16). This meant eating a lot of humble pie, but that's exactly the diet I needed since I was in the wrong. This goes hand in hand with a related principle.

Make Restitution if Necessary.

Sometimes our wrongs inflict terrible damage on others, or at least create substantial problems for them. As a part of restoring our integrity, we need to do whatever we can to repair the damage. This isn't always possible, but we should at least try.

For instance, if you've taken money, abused expense reports, or mishandled funds in some other way, you should repay it—even if it costs you dearly. If you have unjustly damaged someone's career prospects or spread lies about them, you should set the record straight. If you have harmed relationships, you should put in the time and energy necessary to promote healing and reconciliation.

Speaking of relationships, if you're involved in sexual immorality and you've decided to repent of that, you need to take radical steps to break things off. Find another job. Move to another city. Do whatever it takes to get far away and stay away from the person and circumstances in which you've been involved. Sexual liaisons are like weeds: They won't die unless you pull them up by their roots.

When It's Appropriate to Do So, Move On.

Once you've acknowledged your wrongdoing and done what you can to heal the damage, there comes a point when you need to put the past behind you and get on with your life. Obviously, you don't want to rush off and leave unfinished business that will come back to haunt you later. On the other hand, though, you don't want to let your mistakes become a permanent disability to your growth.

I can't say exactly when the time to move on is. But I know that God doesn't put people on the shelf—certainly not those who face their sins squarely. Having received His gracious pardon, and having done what they can to make it up to others who have been wronged, they open a new chapter in their lives and walk on.

Think of how many biblical characters failed in their integrity, repented, and were restored by God to a place of useful service. Moses committed murder, yet God used him to lead Israel. Rahab was a harlot, yet she turned to God and is remembered as one of God's people to this day. Paul was the chief of sinners, he says, but became an example of God's gracious empowering of a human being for His purposes. Peter denied Christ, yet became one of the pillars of the early Church.

Obviously it would be preferable to avoid sinning in the first place. It would save us so much grief. But the point is that God can overcome our failures and, if we'll allow Him, restore us to a place of integrity.

Of course, we can't escape the long-term consequences of our choices. Sexual immorality may have left us divorced or pregnant. Lies may have cost us a career. Chuck Colson's obstruction of justice landed him in jail. We shouldn't expect to be free of such ramifications and blithely return to our former way of life. These are costs of sin that we must pay. Yet the grace of God is such that He helps us as we pay them. He walks with us as we journey out of the swamp into which we have fallen. As Paul wrote (2 Corinthians 12:9-10):

> He has said to me, "My grace is sufficient for you, for power is perfected in weakness." Most gladly, therefore, I will rather boast about my weaknesses, that the power of Christ may dwell in me. Therefore I am well

content with weaknesses, with insults, with distresses, with persecutions, with difficulties, for Christ's sake; for when I am weak, then I am strong.

This amazing statement tells us that while we should be active to reclaim our integrity, we need not be so concerned with our reputation and image. Sure, we'd all like to be regarded as a person whose entire life biblically has been beyond reproach. When we fall, one of our biggest concerns is how it will affect the way others regard us. That worry should concern us very little. Our chief concern should be whether others can see Christ in us as a result of our failure.

Again, consider Chuck Colson. Invariably he is connected in people's minds with Watergate, the biggest political scandal in the history of our country. He's not known as Colson the lawyer, or Colson the former special counsel to the President, or even Colson the Christian writer and thinker. No, he's remembered as Colson the Watergate conspirator, Colson the hatchet man, Colson the White House felon. And yet, his very notoriety has given him an unusual entrée for the gospel, because he is also regarded as Colson, the *born again* figure of Watergate. "When I am weak, then I am strong," Paul says.

So don't live in shame the rest of your life. If you've truly dealt with your sins before God and those you've wronged, then live the truth. Live as a forgiven sinner, as an example of Christ's grace.

It's imperative that you deal with sin in your life, or you will fall ever deeper into moral ruin. How you handle ethical mistakes is as much a part of your integrity as not making them in the first place. Remember, we all can grow through failure. God's grace can overcome our weakness, and He always rewards our obedience. In the next chapter we will look at the long-term considerations of our integrity.

CHAPTER FIFTEEN

Keeping Your Edge Razor Sharp!

Here are habits to help you reinforce your commitment to integrity.

B y now it should be obvious that integrity is not a commodity that can be purchased and kept on an as-needed basis with your other office supplies. It's not a credential like a graduate degree or professional certification that can be acquired and hung on the wall to impress and reassure visitors. Nor is it an inherited trait, like intelligence or baldness, that some have and some don't.

Integrity *is* an attitude and a way of life that you choose to cultivate. It grows out of a set of fundamental beliefs, as we have seen. And it is maintained over the long term by a set of reinforcing habits. Let me mention four that I believe will prove especially helpful.

CULTIVATE INTIMACY WITH GOD

Early in the book we looked at Psalm 15, where David basically asks, "Who gets to enjoy a close, intimate relationship with God?" Recall the answer (verse 2): "He who walks with integrity, and works righteousness, and speaks truth in his heart." So intimacy with God is largely the result of living with integrity. Yet the reverse is true as well: Integrity is largely the product of growing intimate with God.

By way of analogy, think about two people who have been married for years. If they've worked at their marriage and taken steps to know each other intimately, their personalities have slowly started to rub off on each other, and in many ways they begin to resemble one another. That sharing of mannerisms, habits, and thoughts is the product of their intimacy. Yet at the same time, the more they have in common, the deeper their relationship grows.

The same principle can apply to your relationship with God. As you spend time with Him, you'll become like Him. Since He is a Holy God, you'll be stimulated to develop holiness and purity within yourself. Yet as you do, you'll grow ever closer to your Lord, as we see from Psalm 15. It's a cycle of spiritual growth, but you must *choose* to enter the cycle.

How you enter it and stay in it is also something you'll need to decide. There are plenty of books and other guides available that describe how to worship God each day and to feed on His Word. Some even provide day-by-day guides to help you along. Find an approach that seems to work best for you and have at it!

Let me add that I'm struck with the uniqueness of each person's relationship with God. No two are exactly alike, though obviously all Christians have much in common in their spiritual lives. I can't give you *the* method for nurturing intimacy with God, anymore than I can pinpoint exactly how you and your spouse could become intimate. Nevertheless, I offer three observations.

First, people become intimate with God as they *open themselves up to Him.* It's true that God already knows everything about us. But that shouldn't preclude us from revealing ourselves to Him: telling Him about ourselves, about the secret things in our hearts, minds, and feelings that no one else knows, about the hurts and disappointments, the fears and doubts, the hopes and desires, the joys and victories. God is a person, and we need to relate to Him as a person, not as some impersonal force that must be cajoled or placated.

Second, people who become intimate with God *center their understanding of God and His will around the Bible.* Are you ever amazed at any of the weird and contradictory things people parade under the banner of being God's will? They are so out of character with what we know of God from Scripture that they just have to be off base.

The way to avoid falling into that lunatic fringe is to let the Bible inform your understanding of who God is and what He wants done. The Bible is God's written revelation about Himself. It is the best objective source that we have to comprehend what this divine Person is like, and what He wants to see happen in our lives.

Of course, I'm not suggesting that you substitute Bible study, knowledge, or familiarity for a real, vital fellowship with God Himself. The Bible is intended to be a means to that end, not the end itself. So avoid knowing only the Book, and go on to know the Author of the Book—intimately.

Third, people who become intimate with God do so because their *relationship to Him is nourished frequently and goes on continually.* I'm not suggesting that there's a certain time early every morning when you have to be in the Word and in prayer. Many have found that to be helpful. But many others (about whom we don't often hear) find that doesn't work for them. They are not "morning people," or perhaps they have other responsibilities at that hour.

The time of day is not important, the regularity is. It's so foolish to let the busyness of work, family, and social obligations crowd out time alone with God. The relationship simply can't grow, anymore than one's relationship with his spouse can grow unless they spend frequent time alone together. So make up your mind that your schedule will set aside a special time with God *regularly.* But don't leave it at that.

Remember that God goes with you into your day. So maintain communication with Him through prayer—silent prayer when necessary—as you confront the different experiences and situations of your day. Seek His help, His wisdom, and His grace to handle life as it comes.

LEARN HOW TO FIGHT ON YOUR KNEES

Maintaining integrity is a spiritual battle. You face the sinful desires of your own flesh, the seductive temptations of a sinful world system, and worst of all, the subtle, powerful onslaughts of Satan, who prowls about like a hungry lion, looking for someone to devour (1 Peter 5:8).

These are formidable enemies! To overcome them you'll have to use more than your own human resources. You'll have to enlist God's power to prevail. And that requires a concentrated, dedicated prayer life. It's a cliché, but it's also true: Prayer does not prepare us for the battle; prayer *is* the battle.

Now you may be thinking that I'm suggesting you rise each day at 4:00 a.m. and be on your knees for two hours. I doubt that's going to happen—though if it did, we might see some amazing things as a result of the unleashing of God's power. In some countries, like Korea, there *are* believers who come together before dawn to pray. Some even spend all night in prayer. As a result they see some incredible spiritual victories taking place. But I'm realistic enough to know that, for most of us, it's good if we can consistently squeeze in five, ten, or even fifteen minutes of concentrated, uninterrupted time in prayer. If you've never attained to even that much, I suggest you set a goal for yourself to pray for ten minutes a day, three days a week. You can gradually increase that goal over time, but start with something realistic.

As you pray, bring before the Lord any spiritual or moral failures or sins that you have committed. Be sure you include things that you should have done but didn't, as well as those you shouldn't have done but did. Sin needs to be dealt with before you can reestablish intimacy with God. It needs to be admitted by you and forgiven by Him.

Then review the relationships you have with the people in your life: your spouse and family, close friends, associates at work, boss, subordinates, and others with whom you have regular contact. Where is there a conflict that needs to be resolved? Where is there an injury that needs to be healed? Where is there a need that ought to be met? Ask God to point out appropriate responses you should be making in these various relationships.

In addition, pray specifically and with determination about the places in your life where you face particular moral danger or temptation. Is there a deception you are being asked to fabricate? Is there an injustice you could prevent? Is there some money or possession that you're tempted to covet? Is there a sexual temptation lurking? Is there any other situation where you're being asked to compromise your integrity? Such matters need to be discussed before God, and you need to ask for His wisdom and His power to overcome evil with good.

If there is one single strategy that Satan uses to disrupt our spiritual condition more than any other, it is to keep us from prayer. Don't let him succeed in undercutting your effectiveness for God. Make your prayer time a sacred priority. It's not a luxury, it's a necessity!

CULTIVATE A BALANCED LIFE

Another enemy that threatens our integrity is imbalance, particularly in relation to work. Earlier in the book I pointed out that, for many of us, work takes only a third to a half of our time, but it takes ninety-five percent of our emotional energy. In that sense work becomes an idol: It defines our self-worth, becomes the controlling center of our life, and is the last to go among our priorities.

If career success has become our god, then Christ cannot be our Lord. And if that happens we're extremely vulnerable to compromise. If idle hands are the devil's workshop, then overly busy hands are his recreation. He loves to see people too busy to take time for God, too hurried to give any thought to the moral and ethical dimensions of what they're doing.

Our only defense is to set limits on work and keep it in proper perspective with the rest of life. Recall that God desires us to be faithful to Him in five major areas: our personal and spiritual life, family, work, church, and community. We need to balance our commitments in these areas in such a way that we honor God in all five. Doing so will take us a long way toward balancing our use of emotional energy. And that, in turn, will help to safeguard our integrity.

COMMIT YOURSELF TO A GROUP OF PEERS

Too many of us are lone rangers, mavericking our way through life without ever answering to anyone for the moral and ethical choices we make. At the same time, too many others of us feel an ethical loneliness—a sense that we're the only ones who value what we value and believe as we believe. No one else seems to quite understand.

I believe that if you are independent or isolated, you can have your needs met by meeting regularly with a group of peers who know you, know your world, and are committed to applying biblical principles to the tough issues you face. There are probably anywhere from two to twelve others in your network who would fit this category. You may not even realize it! Why not come together for discussion and see if there's a helpful chemistry?

One of the chief values of such a peer group, assuming it's set up properly, is encouragement and accountability. Somehow when we know that others stand behind us to cheer us on, as well as look over our shoulder to review what we do, it helps us follow through on our commitments in a way we never could alone. Furthermore, the collective wisdom of such a group is ideal for problem solving and decision making.

I recommend that you recruit such a discussion group from your network of peers. Focus on applying God's truths to the tough, practical issues you face every day. I wouldn't suggest a lecture format; that has its place, but this needs to be an interactive group, a discussion in which everyone gets involved in the process. Discussion materials for this book begin on page 213. Our goal is not to get you to discuss our books, but rather to get you to discuss *your life* with your peers and to see God's Word make a real difference in the way you live.

That's why I encourage you to go on into the study guide. You'll find exercises there that Bill and I have developed to help you cultivate biblical integrity. We think that your having read this far will help to orient your thinking in the right direction. But to really experience life-change, you'll need to take active, practical steps in the coming days. The study guide will help you take those steps in a coordinated, well-paced way.

YOU CAN MAKE A DIFFERENCE

In chapter 2, I described the tragic mudslide that is slowly squeezing the moral and spiritual life out of our society. On every hand, it seems, people are giving way to greed, selfish ambition, and momentary pleasure. From one point of view, it's a dark day in which to be living, a time like the one described at the end of the book of Judges, when "everyone did what was right in his own eyes" (21:25).

Yet this need not be the end of the story. As we have seen in the preceding chapters, it *is* possible—and preferable—to stand firm for God, to maintain biblical integrity, to keep one's ethical edge razor sharp. Not easy, but certainly possible.

In that case, this day of massive moral failure is also a day of unparalleled opportunity—to live distinctively for Christ "in the midst of a crooked and perverse generation" (Philippians 2:15). This is a day when people of integrity can shine like stars and exert profound moral leadership. So starved are people today for ethical models and moral champions that they will follow anyone who appears to know what is right and true.

Will others follow you? Are your lifestyle and workstyle so unique and distinctive that your coworkers wonder why? Or have you accepted moral mediocrity and become morally camouflaged at work—indistinguishable from those who care nothing for Christ and His values?

CHAPTER SIXTEEN

You'll Have Your Day in Court

*We all demand justice, and
someday we'll have it!*

One of the important principles of life strongly reinforced by the workplace is that there are consequences to one's behavior. Perhaps you're in an industry
where periodically you receive a performance review from
your boss. It's usually a tense time because you realize that
pay raises, preferential treatment, and career opportunities
may be riding on the outcome.

Likewise, professional athletes receive constant feedback from coaches, and often there are monetary incentives
tied to their performance. Doctors and lawyers have a less
formal means of evaluation, though there are professional
and governmental bodies looking over their shoulders,
ready to step in when there's a problem.

In the military, the other pilots and I went through
seemingly endless checks and performance reviews. Sometimes it seemed like every sneeze had to be recorded and
entered into our files. When it came time for promotions
and raises, the commanding officers would review that data
and use it to determine the outcome. If things didn't go
quite like you expected them, you might resent it, but that

was too bad. That was the way the system worked.

It's the way life in general works, too. There are consequences to our actions and decisions. Very rarely do we actually "get away" with anything. There is always some means of accountability, whether it's the formal review of a superior or the more informal consequences related to things like self-respect, friendships, or our feelings.

So this should come as no surprise: Just as there are consequences here and now for the work we do and the way we do it, there will also be ultimate, eternal consequences before God. The principle is one of accountability. Though we often hear that concept taught in terms of what's going to happen to us in this life, we rarely hear it connected with the eternal consequences of our work. But it's an important truth to understand, particularly in the matter of integrity.

WE MUST ALL APPEAR BEFORE CHRIST

Accountability is not a biblical term, but it is a biblical principle. You won't find any words translated "accountability," but you can find plenty of instances where the principle is at work. For instance, we saw in chapter 4 the outcome of the naive youth in Proverbs 7. One of the powerful lessons is that there are always consequences to our actions. In his case, they were tragic.

In the parable of the talents in Matthew 25, three managers are given responsibilities by their master. Eventually he reviews their work and rewards them accordingly. To the first two he pronounces "Well done," increases their responsibilities, and welcomes them to a new level of intimacy with the words, "Enter into the joy of your master"! But with the third manager, who has been profligate, he flies into a rage and calls him wicked and lazy. He also has him banished. The manager's irresponsibility brings him permanent grief and regret. While the outcome for the first two is unbelievably positive, that of the third manager is tragically severe.

It's an ancient principle that there are consequences to our choices and a built-in accountability to life. Proverbs 22:8 warns, "He who sows iniquity will reap vanity, and the rod of his fury will perish." Paul picks up on this metaphor in Galatians 6:7-8 (he uses it in a different context in 2 Corinthians 9:6):

> Do not be deceived, God is not mocked; for whatever a man sows, this he will also reap. For the one who sows to his own flesh shall from the flesh reap corruption, but the one who sows to the Spirit shall from the Spirit reap eternal life.

It's easy to see that accountability is a basic principle of life taught by the Bible. However, we need to make an important distinction when we talk about eternal accountability before God. Every human is and will be judged by God. Indeed, the theologically correct way to say that is that every one of us already stands under the judgment and condemnation of the Holy God for our sin. As Paul states in Romans 2:11-12:

> For there is no partiality with God. For all who have sinned without the Law will also perish without the Law; and all who have sinned under the Law will be judged by the Law.

That's why the person who places faith in Christ's death and receives His forgiveness for sin should be so grateful. He lives under God's grace—free from that ultimate and terrible judgment (Romans 8:1): "There is therefore now no condemnation for those who are in Christ Jesus."

So there is a primary accountability in terms of salvation. Those who ignore or reject God's provision for it in Christ will die and suffer the eternal consequences of having said no to God. They will go to hell. By contrast, those who respond to Christ's invitation of life will die but enjoy the eternal benefits of living with Him. The Bible describes this outcome as Heaven.

Does your work and your integrity on the job affect whether you will end up in Heaven or hell? No, not directly. What happens after you die depends, from the human perspective, entirely on whether you accept or reject Jesus Christ. If you've responded to His offer of salvation, then you'll meet Him someday in Heaven. If you haven't, I urge you to do so right now. Your final, eternal destiny is at stake.

But let's assume that you are trusting Christ for your salvation, that you have responded to Him, that you are what we call a Christian. You're home free, right? I mean, if you've got your salvation, if you're Heaven-bound, then you can relax and live out your days with relative abandon. The pressure's off. You've got your "fire insurance," and that's what counts, right?

Unfortunately, too many Christians act as if they believe that way, whether they openly admit it or not. I hope you're not in that category. If you are, you'll be sorely shocked someday! For the truth is that there will be accountability for Christians someday before Christ. What we do now will be evaluated by Him in Heaven someday, and that means there are eternal consequences to our earthly behavior, even as Christians. Our ultimate salvation won't be on the line, but some aspect of the life we live with God for eternity will be affected.

Paul warns believers that a day of accountability is coming (2 Corinthians 5:10):

For we must all appear before the judgment seat of
Christ, that each one may be recompensed for his
deeds in the body, according to what he has done,
whether good or bad.

All here refers to all believers. The "judgment seat"
is a curious term. Probably the idea of a courtroom enters
your mind, and that's not far off the mark. In the United
States, you can picture the judgment seat as the table where
the defendant sits. In the British courts, one would call it
the dock.

To really understand the image here, you have to go
back about 500 years before Paul's letter to the Corinthians
to the golden age of Athens. At that time Athens boasted
some 150,000 inhabitants. About forty times a year, free
male citizens met (sometimes by coercion) in general
assembly at the Pnyx, a natural amphitheater west of town.
The Pnyx could seat a full house of 18,000, no doubt considerably more standing.

Lacking microphones and electronic amplification, a
speaker had to rely on his lungs and oratorical skills to be
heard, as well as on the natural reverberations of the arena
and the cooperation of the crowd. His major advantage was
the speaker's podium facing the hillside. This raised platform, which still stands, elevated him to a position of prom-
inence from which he could command attention and have
his say. The Greek word for this platform is *bema*—the same
word Paul uses in 2 Corinthians 5.

Of course, by the time of Paul, Athenian glory (and
democracy) had vanished, and *bema* referred to any raised
place where one could address a crowd. Such platforms
were certainly a part of the judicial system. They were the
tribunals at which a prisoner stood to make his defense and
hear the verdict. So the word is technically translated cor-

rectly as "judgment seat," but the image is much greater.

Perhaps you've been wronged somewhere along the way, and you cried, "I'll have my day in court!" Paul is saying that, as a Christian, you'll have your day in court, in the ultimate Court of God. Like an Athenian orator, you'll get to stand before the assembled throng of all believers, and before Christ as the final judge. There, your life will be reviewed, and you'll get to have your say.

We can't imagine how that review will work or what will be revealed. Maybe a movie or videotape of our lives will be shown. Perhaps our own memories will be played back. Who knows? We do know that justice will be done. I suspect that all the hurts, injuries, and problems that never got resolved here will be settled there. You'll finally get to tell your side of the story. And Christ will work it all out.

Furthermore, Paul says that we will be "recompensed" for our deeds whether good or bad. In other words, we'll be fairly evaluated by God and receive either rewards or punishments, depending on what we've done in our lives. We don't know exactly what form those rewards or punishments will take, but one thing is clear: There are definite, tangible, eternal consequences to what we do right here, right now.

If that is so, then perhaps most of those judgments *will pertain to your work*. In Ephesians 6 Paul urges employees to obey their masters, doing good work with excellence. Here's why (verse 8): "Knowing that whatever good thing each one does, this he will receive back from the Lord, whether slave or free." A similar idea is given in Colossians 3:23-25:

> Whatever you do, do your work heartily, as for the
> Lord rather than for men; knowing that from the Lord
> you will receive the reward of the inheritance. It is the

Lord Christ whom you serve. For he who does wrong will receive the consequences of the wrong which he has done, and that without partiality.

By the way, Paul also warns employers, pointing out that they have an employer in Heaven (Ephesians 6:9, Colossians 4:1).

Most of us spend at least a third of our waking hours at work. If you add in commuting, work-related tasks, and overtime, we may spend half of our time or more involved with work. I think it's safe to assume then that up to half of the final evaluation will pertain to work. Don't be like the naive youth in Proverbs 7 who was tricked into thinking there would be no consequences to compromise. On the other hand, remember that your integrity will be rewarded!

LIVING IN LIGHT OF ETERNITY

I don't know how it impacts you to know that your work today will someday be reviewed before Christ. It hits me pretty solidly, and it makes me want to stop and consider what I'm doing. I think that's why God tells us that a day of accounting will come. Specifically, He may want to promote several things in us.

A Healthy Fear of the Lord

Most of us work with a little thought lurking somewhere in the back of our minds: "If I don't do this job well, I'm going to get fired." A friend of mine calls this a low-voltage tension. It's actually a healthy fear of our employer. That tension should rarely if ever be amplified to a high-voltage terror of unemployment; we couldn't function properly if it were. But it should motivate us to get our work done.

The idea that we'll stand before God someday and

account for our lives should create a similar low-voltage tension in the way we live. We should act with the certainty that what we do and how we do it will be reviewed by Christ. The Bible calls this the "fear of God."

Positive Change

If you really believe that you'll stand before Christ someday, then you'll likely want to take action right away to clean up your life. All of us could stand some improvements in our character. This idea of an ultimate accountability should motivate us to take responsibility for change.

Obviously you can't change everything at once. Real change happens over time, so you have to be patient and realistic. But you can start taking small steps in a few areas right now. What you don't want to do is live carelessly, with no sense of accountability. You'll regret it when you stand before Christ. (See 1 Corinthians 3:12-15.)

Motivation to Do Good Work

Earlier in the book I outlined the dignity and value that your everyday work has before God. You are a coworker with Him to accomplish His purposes in the world and to meet the needs of people. This should encourage you in what you do and send you to work with a real motivation to do your job "as unto the Lord."

But we have an additional motivation to work with excellence: you'll be rewarded for it. I don't know exactly how. But inasmuch as God is the One giving out the prizes, I suspect they will be beyond any trophy or plaque or bonus we could receive here on earth.

I believe the spirit of the Bible's teaching is that, in view of the judgment seat of Christ, we should do the following: obey the authority of our employers; do the very best job we can on behalf of the company's objectives; treat coworkers with respect and fairness and customers with dignity and honesty; resolve conflicts as best we can in a healthy manner; use our income wisely and not squander it on selfish comforts and conveniences; respect company property; give an honest day's labor for our wages; and pray for all those we work with. Many more behaviors could be listed, but you get the point. A performance review is awaiting us and the evaluator is Christ. We need to work with an eye toward pleasing Him.

Motivation Toward Clean Living

Not only should our workstyle honor God, our lifestyle needs to honor Him, too. So often we live as if no one is watching and we'll never get caught. But that's a lie! Someone *is* watching, and we *will* be asked about our behavior. It's a scary thing in some ways!

Perhaps a rule of thumb to adopt as we make moral choices is that we'll never do anything privately that we'd be ashamed to have known publicly. Obviously there are reasons to keep some things private: to protect the confidences of others, to avoid misunderstandings, to keep competition fair, to keep people from getting hurt. But in Heaven, it sounds like there will be no secrets anymore. It will be appropriate to open the files and air out the closets. What surprises there will be!

Let me underscore that no one has any idea what the exact nature of the judgment seat of Christ will be. Perhaps many things will be kept quiet; maybe every last moment of our lives will be laid bare. This is certain: We will be held accountable for the way we have lived. Knowing that we will look directly into the eyes of the One who bore all of our sins and knows us through and through, and that He will look back into our eyes and speak in our hearing whatever conclusion He wants to pronounce on our earthly existence, ought to make a radical difference in us right now.

As you conclude this book, I challenge you to make up your mind that, no matter how others around you choose to live, you at least will live for Christ. This needs to be the nonnegotiable commitment on which your ethics and values are based. Sure you may have blown it, but it's never too late to start doing what is right. You'll never be perfect—at least not in this life—but God understands that, and He asks only that you faithfully pursue Christlikeness, not that you master it.

Someday you and I will stand before our Lord, and He will assess the extent to which we have honored His will and His values in our lives and in our work. Can there possibly be *anything* we could have right now—riches, acclaim, prestige, power, even friends or family—that would be so valuable and so worth having that it could outweigh His approval, His pronouncement of "well done"? Could *anything* be worth more than that?

I don't think so. I hope and pray you don't either. So let's dedicate ourselves to lives of integrity and a passion for moral excellence. It seems an understatement when God promises that in doing so "there is *great* reward" (Psalm 19:11, emphasis added)!

Sharpening Your Edge:

A Manual for Growth

The material that follows is a six-part manual to help you apply the principles in this book to your life. There's no question that while we retain very little of what we read, we retain nearly all of what we do. In the sessions that follow, you'll *do* far more than you'll read!

Here's how to gain the most from this material.

USE IT WITH A GROUP

We find that small discussion groups are an ideal way to apply biblical truth to life. That's why we've designed this for discussion, not just self-study. We strongly encourage you to interact with a group of your friends using this manual. To have an effective group, you'll need to do several things:

1. Limit the group to six or eight people. If you have nine or more, we recommend splitting into two groups.

2. Make sure each participant has a copy of this book.

3. Be clear as to the time and place for the discussion.

4. Clarify expectations before you begin meeting. Every-

one should agree on the purpose of the group and the level of commitment to it.

5. Set a termination date for the group, or at least for using this book. Don't ask people to make open-ended commitments.

6. Appoint a discussion leader. This person is not a teacher, but someone who can facilitate a healthy group interaction.

7. Keep the discussion focused. The questions and material in this guide have been designed very carefully to help you think and talk about important issues. Don't get sidetracked. Encourage *everyone* to participate. This is a discussion, not a lecture or a platform for one person's point of view.

8. Come prepared to discuss. The preparation involved is minimal. Each session corresponds to sections of the book, so reading the material ahead of time will help. However, someone can easily participate in the discussion even if that person hasn't read the book.

9. We haven't left much space in this guide to write notes, so you may find it helpful to record answers to some questions in a separate notebook or journal. This will prove especially helpful for the exercises that require extended responses and reflection.

10. Some of the questions in this guide ask for honest self-disclosure. To make this kind of vulnerability possible and healthy, you must agree to maintain strict confidences, to avoid judgment, and to strive for honesty even when it's uncomfortable.

SUGGESTIONS FOR GROUP LEADERS

You have an important role to play in making this experience helpful for everyone. In any group situation, someone's got to get things rolling and keep things moving. That's your job! If you do it well, the other natural dynamics of the group process will take care of everything else.

1. Come prepared. At a minimum, this involves reading the book and previewing the particular session that your group will cover. Doing so will give you confidence and a sense of where things are headed during the discussion. Moreover, your preparation sets a vital example for the other participants. It shows them how seriously you take the group, and therefore, how seriously they should take it.

2. Your goal is to keep a lively discussion going. You can do that by probing people's responses, asking for clarification, sometimes bringing up an opposite idea or a possible objection (playing the devil's advocate). Of course, others in the group should be encouraged to do the same. Whatever you do, avoid "teaching" the content of the book.

3. Don't let someone dominate the group with his or her opinions or personality. Try to get all the participants— especially shy or quiet ones—to say at least one or two things at each session.

4. Keep track of the time. Before the group meets, think through how much time should be allotted to each section of the session. That way you can keep things moving. We've designed each session to have resolution and completion, so if the last few questions or exercises are not covered, people may feel frustrated. By the way, the ideal length of time for a discussion is an hour to an hour and fifteen minutes.

5. End the discussion on time. People have other responsibilities and commitments. If the session lasts too long, they may develop a negative attitude toward the group. By contrast, cutting off a lively interaction will bring everyone back with enthusiasm. Our rule is, "Leave them longing, not loathing!"

THIS GUIDE CAN BE USED FOR SELF-STUDY

Discussion groups won't work for everyone. That's okay. You can still enjoy valuable benefits from this guide even in self-study. Just make a couple of adjustments.

1. You'll have to be much more self-disciplined because you won't have the built-in accountability of a group. We recommend that you determine a specific time and place to study. Then put that in your appointment book so you won't crowd it out with other commitments.

2. Since you won't have a group to discuss the material with, you'll spend a great deal of effort in personal reflection and thought. Writing (or taping) will replace discussing. However, you should seek opportunities to discuss your ideas with others—coworkers, your spouse, other Christians in your network. These people will be invaluable in helping you gain perspective and offering you objective feedback, even though they will participate on an informal basis.

Session 1

*In this session you'll examine
the issues of cheating and stealing on the job,
and decide how to avoid them.*

PART ONE

SUGGESTED TIME: 20 MINUTES

Here are some common ways that workers cheat and steal on the job:

- Pilfering supplies
- Calling in sick when not sick
- Overstating expenses on expense forms
- Overpricing products
- Copying copyrighted software

1. What additional ways can you think of in which people cheat and steal at work? Add these to the list above.

2. What kinds of cheating and stealing are common problems where you work or in your industry?

3. What do you think people hope to gain by cheating or stealing on the job?

PART TWO
SUGGESTED TIME: 25 MINUTES

4. Read Ephesians 4:28: "Let him who steals steal no longer; but rather let him labor, performing with his own hands what is good, in order that he may have something to share with him who has need."

   This verse affirms the value of honest work. What do you think is the effect of honest labor on each of the following?

   - The worker himself
   - His family
   - His friends
   - His employer
   - His coworkers
   - His customers
   - His community

5. If honesty were the hallmark of your workplace, what would be different?

6. What specific steps can you take to promote honesty where you work?

PART THREE
SUGGESTED TIME: 10 MINUTES

I want you to get the most you can from this book and the sessions that follow. But a lot depends on you, and what you plan to gain from this experience. Reflect for a few moments on how you would complete the statement at the top of the following page, then write your response in the space provided.

As a result of going through this book and the exercises in this study guide, I'd like to make the following changes in my life:

ON YOUR OWN

The following exercises are optional, and should be completed on your own if you are using this guide with a discussion group. I encourage you to complete these, as an additional way to apply biblical principles to your own life.

1. Memorize Ephesians 4:28 (see preceding page).

2. Ask two or three coworkers the following questions:

a. What are some common forms of cheating or stealing in our kind of work?

b. Why should someone even try to remain honest when others are dishonest?

c. How could we encourage honesty among our coworkers?

3. In light of this session, review chapter 5, "H—Honesty."

4. In preparation for session 2, read chapter 6, "O—Obey Authority."

Session 2

*In this session you'll consider
obedience to authority.*

PART ONE

SUGGESTED TIME: 30 MINUTES

In chapter 14, "Picking Up the Pieces," I describe a situation that happened to me when I was going through flight training. Unfortunately, I lost my cool and showed disrespect for my instructor's authority. Reread that story (it begins on page 181) and then discuss the following questions.

1. This incident didn't happen without reason. It came as a result of many factors that had been building over time. What do you think were some of those factors?

2. How do you think I could have handled that situation differently?

3 Have you ever been in a situation similar to the one I describe, especially where you work? What did you do, and why?

PART TWO

SUGGESTED TIME: 25 MINUTES

4. Read Titus 2:9-10 (NIV): "Teach slaves to be subject to their masters in everything, to try to please them, not to talk back to them, and not to steal from them, but to show that they can be fully trusted, so that in every way they will make the teaching about God our Savior attractive."

    This verse teaches that employees should be obedient to their employers. What are some ways that you can respect the authority of your employer?

5. Are there things that your employer asks you to do that you're tempted not to do? What steps can you take that will help you follow through with his orders?

ʠ According to Titus 2:9-10, our behavior on the job should "make the teaching about God our Savior attractive." In other words, God's reputation is on the line in the way we obey our bosses. How could you make your faith attractive to your boss through the way you work? What would make the greatest impression on him?

ON YOUR OWN

1. Memorize Titus 2:9-10 above.

2. Review your memorization of Ephesians 4:28.

3. Invite your boss to lunch or have a conference with him in order to discuss ways that you can be a better employee.

4. If you are not already doing so, get in the habit of praying regularly for your boss or supervisor—for his spiritual, emotional, and physical needs.

5. In light of this session, review chapter 6, "O—Obey Authority."

6. In preparation for the next session, read chapter 7, "N—No Deception."

Session 3

*In this session you'll consider the problem of
lying and look at ways to tell the truth instead.*

PART ONE

SUGGESTED TIME: 25 MINUTES

The following survey is adapted from "Lies, Damn Lies,
and Statistics," by Richard Morin (*The Washington Post
Magazine*, December 27, 1987). Circle the responses that
apply to you.

1. Which do you think you are?
   Basically honest   Basically dishonest

2. Generally speaking, how does your honesty today
   compare to your honesty ten years ago?
   More honest   Less honest   About the same

3. Following are a few reasons for lying. Decide how
   often you lie for each reason.

   a. To cover up something you did wrong
   Frequently   Sometimes   Hardly ever   Never

b. To make yourself seem more important
Frequently   Sometimes   Hardly ever   Never

c. To avoid an unpleasant social situation
Frequently   Sometimes   Hardly ever   Never

d. Because it seems easier to lie than to tell the truth
Frequently   Sometimes   Hardly ever   Never

e. To get ahead at work
Frequently   Sometimes   Hardly ever   Never

f. To avoid hurting someone's feelings
Frequently   Sometimes   Hardly ever   Never

g. To avoid embarrassment
Frequently   Sometimes   Hardly ever   Never

4. Some people feel there are two basic kinds of lies. The first kind is "little white lies," which are not meant to harm anyone. The other kind is serious lies that conceal wrongdoing and can cause a lot of harm.

a. Have you ever told a white lie?   Yes   No

b. How often would you say that you tell white lies?
A great deal   A fair amount   Hardly ever

c. Do you think it is usually right or usually wrong to tell a white lie?   Usually right   Usually wrong

5. Following are some white lies that people often tell. Have you ever told a white lie similar to each one mentioned?

a. Telling someone you didn't want to see, "How nice to see you." Yes No

b. Telling a store, "The check bounced because my bank has my account all messed up." Yes No

c. Telling someone who has invited you to a social function, "We can't make it; we've made other plans." Yes No

d. Telling someone you did better in school than you really did. Yes No

e. Telling someone you made more money than you actually did. Yes No

f. Telling a friend you weighed less than you actually did. Yes No

g. Lying about your age. Yes No

h. Telling someone you'd rather not see again, "We really must get together sometime." Yes No

i. Telling someone asking for money, "I'm a little strapped financially right now." Yes No

j. Telling someone who has called for someone else in the office, "He's not here right now." Yes No

6. Have you ever told a serious lie? Yes No

7. How frequently would you say that you tell serious lies?
   A great deal   A fair amount   Hardly ever

8. Do you feel that when you tell a lie the person believes you?

Always   Sometimes   Never

9. When you're caught in a lie, how often do you tell another lie to cover up?

Frequently   Sometimes   Hardly ever   Never

10. Do you agree or disagree with the idea that sometimes you just *have* to lie?

Agree   Disagree

11. Do you believe that you are less honest or more honest than most people?

Less honest   More honest

Discussion Questions

1. Do you think people in general are basically honest or basically dishonest? Why?

2. Nearly everyone believes that he is more honest than most people. (What was *your* answer to question 11?) Why do you think that is so? Do you think it's true?

3. As for "little white lies" (question 5), which of the lies listed do you hear a lot? Why do you think people choose to tell these lies rather than the truth?

4. Several reasons for lying are listed in question 3. Which do you think is the most frequent reason? Why is this so prevalent?

PART TWO

Read Ephesians 4:25 and Colossians 3:9: "Therefore, laying aside falsehood, speak truth, each one of you, with his neighbor, for we are members of one another."

"Do not lie to one another, since you laid aside the old self with its evil practices."

5. What reasons do these passages give for telling the truth?

6. What kinds of deception are you tempted to use in the course of your work? What would you gain by being dishonest? What happens if you remain honest?

7. Look back over your responses to the survey in part 1. In general, are you satisfied with your own level of honesty? What steps can you take to improve it?

ON YOUR OWN

1. Memorize Ephesians 4:25 or Colossians 3:9 above.

2. Review your memorization of Ephesians 4:28 and Titus 2:9-10.

3. If you want to get an objective opinion about how honest you are, ask someone who knows you well— perhaps someone who works with you regularly, or your spouse—to complete the survey in part 1 as if the questions were about you. Then discuss the results together

4. Use a concordance to look up verses about lying. How does God view lying? Why?

5. In light of this session, review chapter 7, "N—No Deception."

6. In preparation for the next session, read chapter 8, "E—Encourage Conflict Resolution."

Session 4

*In this session you'll consider
how to encourage resolution of conflict
where you work.*

PART ONE

SUGGESTED TIME: 35 MINUTES

Several conflict situations are described below. Discuss the
following questions for each situation:

- What do you think would be some poor ways for the
people involved to handle the conflict? Explain why.
- What do you think would be some positive ways for
the people involved to resolve the conflict? Explain why.

1. Jim and Shelley work in the media department of a
   medium-size corporation. Their boss has assigned
   them to produce an in-house video for training purposes. Shelley wants Jim to write the script while she
   works on the visuals. But Jim, who is fairly new to the
   company, feels that Shelley should write it, and he
   should work on the visuals, as he feels that is his
   strength. They've already spent two meetings trying
   to work it out, but there is no resolution in sight.

2. Andrew is selling a piece of property. He holds a letter of intent and a deposit from a prospective buyer, an investment firm represented by Allen. For months things have dragged on without closure on the sale. Andrew keeps calling Allen, but he is rarely available. Yet Andrew hears the message that Allen's firm remains "very interested" in the land, and the sale should happen "any day." Now another buyer wants the property, and Andrew has asked Allen's firm to either come to terms or rescind its offer to buy. In response he has received a letter stating that Allen's firm will conclude the sale when it is good and ready, and that it doesn't appreciate Andrew's "pressure tactics."

3. Loraine hired a contractor to build her house. The job went smoothly and Loraine was pleased with the outcome. But a week after she moved in, thunderstorms dumped several inches of water in the area, and Loraine's basement flooded. Since she had specifically discussed the problem of flooding with the contractor before the house was built, she felt that he should come and make whatever changes were necessary, at his own expense. But when she contacted him, he blamed the architect, who in turn blamed the contractor. Neither one wants to accept responsibility or pay for repairs.

4. Helen and Sarah started a software development company. They wrote up an informal agreement that said that if one of them wanted out of the company at any time, the other would have first right to buy her out. Unfortunately things didn't work out. After two years, Sarah decided to leave. So she totalled up what she felt her share in the firm was worth and sent a copy to

Helen. Several days later Sarah was shocked to receive a call from Helen's lawyer threatening a lawsuit if Sarah did not drop her demand for the amount requested and accept a smaller amount instead.

5. Isaac worked on a construction crew. One day his boss asked him to run an errand. The only available vehicle on the site was a new pickup belonging to the owner of the construction company. Isaac drove the pickup on the errand and returned it to the job site. Later in the day the company owner and Isaac's boss came over to him. "What happened to my truck?" the owner asked excitedly. Isaac didn't know what he was talking about. But when the three walked over to where the truck was parked, Isaac saw that one side bore an ugly scrape and a dent. He denied any knowledge of how the damage had occurred, but both the owner and Isaac's boss insisted that Isaac must be lying.

PART TWO
SUGGESTED TIME: 20 MINUTES

6. Read Romans 12:17-18: "Never pay back evil for evil to anyone. Respect what is right in the sight of all men. If possible, so far as it depends on you, be at peace with all men."

a. It's impossible to avoid conflicts, but this verse encourages the peaceful resolution of conflict. Why is it so hard to settle conflicts in a peaceful manner, without doing damage to relationships?

b. Verse 18 indicates that you are responsible only for your side of the argument: "So far as it depends on you." When you're in a conflict with someone else, what steps can you take to try to work things out?

7. Are you facing a conflict at work right now? Perhaps you could describe the situation to your group and discuss ways for you to settle the matter in a healthy, Christlike way.

ON YOUR OWN

1. Memorize Romans 12:17-18 above.

2. Review your memorization of Ephesians 4:28, Titus 2:9-10, and either Ephesians 4:25 or Colossians 3:9.

3. Perhaps you've had a relationship destroyed because of conflict. Consider whether you may need to go back to that person and apologize and/or forgive him in order to resolve the conflict and promote healing.

4. In light of this session, review chapter 8, "E—Encourage Conflict Resolution."

5. In preparation for the next session, read chapter 9, "S—Sexual Fidelity."

Session 5

*In this session you'll consider
the topic of sexual fidelity and
how you can remain morally pure.*

PART ONE

SUGGESTED TIME: 25 MINUTES

Read the following case history and then discuss the questions following it.

One day I was working at my office when I received a call from a woman named Linda. She and her husband had been participants in some programs I taught, so I knew her fairly well, though I had not seen her for a long time. As soon as I picked up the receiver, I could tell that something was desperately wrong. Normally full of energy, Linda's voice sounded leaden and stressed. Indeed, as she spoke, I thought she would burst into tears at any moment.

Realizing that this was a matter too involved to get into on the phone, I complied with her request for an appointment. It struck me as odd that she wanted to come without her husband. I surmised that perhaps their marriage was in trouble. Perhaps Linda's husband wanted out of the marriage and she was seeking counsel. Perhaps her husband had had an affair.

I was dead wrong. It was she who was having an affair. When she told me, my heart ached and my mind began to spin. It seemed incredulous to me. Linda was the last person I would ever expect to get off the track morally. She had been a faithful participant not only in my programs, but also those at her church. While her husband struck me as cold and distant, she was alive and vibrant by contrast. And it appeared to me that she loved him despite his restrained demeanor. How could this have happened?

The story Linda related was simple enough. With her two children in junior high school, she decided to resume her career as a sales representative. Her outgoing personality and quick mind made her a natural in persuading people to buy her product.

Several weeks before our conversation, she had attended a major convention with some of her associates in a distant city. One evening after dinner, the group voted to gather in Gary's room and watch a movie. As a believer, Linda didn't care much for the movie selected by her peers—a rather racy, raunchy adventure story—but she was outvoted.

It was already late when the movie began, and before long various ones in the group left to return to their rooms. Later Linda wondered why she didn't leave, too. By the time the movie ended, she and her roommate and Gary were the only ones left.

A discussion began, and lasted for some time. In the middle of a point that Linda was making, her roommate left to return to their room. Now it was just Linda and Gary. The talk continued. Only it turned to more personal matters, and eventually to deeply private aspects of each other's marriages. One thing led to another, and Linda woke up the next morning in Gary's bed.

The most tragic part of Linda's tale was that upon her return home, she and Gary continued their affair; she said that she was in love with him and wanted to leave her family and pursue her relationship with him. She came to see me only upon the insistence of her husband.

I reasoned with Linda and challenged her to forsake this sinful relationship. Later I met with both her and her husband, but it was to no avail. While I never heard the final outcome, things were definitely headed for a tragedy.

1. What factors do you think might have led to Linda's compromise of her sexual integrity?

2. What mistakes do you think Linda made?

3. Why do you think sexual immorality is so prevalent in our culture?

4. Is sexual temptation and compromise a common element where you work?

PART TWO
SUGGESTED TIME: 20 MINUTES

5. Read 1 Thessalonians 4:3-4: "For this is the will of God, your sanctification; that is, that you abstain from sexual immorality; that each of you know how to possess his own vessel in sanctification and honor."

   This passage exhorts us to strive for sexual purity. What safeguards could you take to maintain your integrity in this area?

6. What obstacles and difficulties might hinder you from keeping yourself pure? How can you handle these?

7. In today's workplace you'll often find yourself dealing with members of the opposite sex. Brainstorm ways that you can keep these relationships healthy and far removed from temptation.

ON YOUR OWN

1. Memorize 1 Thessalonians 4:3-4 above.

2. Review your memorization of Ephesians 4:28, Titus 2:9-10, either Ephesians 4:25 or Colossians 3:9, and Romans 12:17-18.

3. a. If you are married, consider the quality of your relationship with your spouse. Keeping yourself morally pure will depend to a large extent on whether your marriage is healthy and vital. If you struggle with recurring problems in your marriage, seek godly counsel from a pastor or marital counselor. Don't ignore problems in this important relationship!

b. If you are single, consider the quality of your relationships with members of the opposite sex, as well as your sexual life in general. If you find recurring problems here, consult your pastor or a godly counselor. Don't ignore problems in this vital area of your life!

4. In light of this session, review chapter 9, "S—Sexual Fidelity."

5. In preparation for the next session, read chapter 10, "T—Trustworthiness."

Session 6

In this session you'll consider the important quality of trustworthiness, and how you can cultivate faithfulness as an employee. You'll also evaluate what you've learned from this book.

PART ONE

SUGGESTED TIME: 35 MINUTES

Psalm 15:4 describes a trustworthy person: "He swears to his own hurt, and does not change."

1. People today seem to make contingency commitments: They'll do what they promise unless something better comes along. Have you encountered instances of this where you work? Describe a situation.
   Why do you think people break their commitments?

2. What might "swearing to your own hurt" mean if you were faced with one or more of the following situations?

   a. You sign a contract to do some work for someone and then you discover that the job will cost you twice what you contracted for.

233

b. You agree to pay a friend back in installments for a loan and then you lose your job.

c. You promise to finish a work project over the weekend, shortly before your best friends invite you to their lakehouse.

d. You accept a job based on a certain job description, knowing that one of the responsibilities described is something you dislike

e. You make a commitment to contribute a certain amount of money to your church or other organization, but a business deal you thought would go through doesn't.

f. Employees under you complain about a policy or procedure that isn't working, and that only you can change, but months later, nothing is being done to change the situation.

3. Have you made a commitment that you're having trouble honoring? What steps can you take to demonstrate faithfulness in the situation?

PART TWO

SUGGESTED TIME: 20 MINUTES

You would be wise to complete the evaluation form on pages 237-238 as a way of analyzing what you've gained from this book and these sessions. Then discuss the following questions with your group:

4. What was the best thing about this group experience?

5. What progress have you actually made toward developing a biblical view of integrity?

6. What one specific way would you especially like to grow in the coming months?

7. Is a discussion group like this one something you'd like to continue in the future? If so, what practical issues or topics would be helpful to study together?

ON YOUR OWN

1. Memorize Psalm 15:4 above.

2. Review your memorization of Ephesians 4:28, Titus 2:9-10, either Ephesians 4:25 or Colossians 3:9, Romans 12:17-18, and 1 Thessalonians 4:3-4.

3. Read *In Search of Faithfulness* by William Diehl.

4. If you have not done so, complete the evaluation form on pages 237-238.

5. In light of this session, review chapter 10, "T—Trustworthiness."

6. Discuss the value of this book and what you've gained from it with someone who knows you well, such as your spouse or a close friend.

Evaluation Form

If you've read this book and worked through all of the exercises in the six sessions in the study guide, you've done a lot of constructive work toward developing a biblical view of integrity. Now complete the job by evaluating your experience.

1. What percentage of the exercises and questions did you complete?

2. If you were part of a discussion group, how many of the group meetings did you participate in?

3. To what extent do you think this experience will make a difference in your life and the quality of your character?

1	2	3	4	5
No Difference				Major Difference

4. Look back at your response to the question asked in part 3 of session 1 (page 215). You hoped to gain something from this experience. Did you?

5. Describe how this experience could have been more helpful.

Bill and I would like to know how this material has affected your life, and how we can improve our resources to be more helpful. Please complete the two statements that follow and send your responses to:

> Doug Sherman
> Career Impact Ministries
> 8201 Cantrell Road, Suite 240
> Little Rock, AR 72207
> 1-800-4-IMPACT

Include your name and address on the page with your responses.

As a result of your book, *Keeping Your Ethical Edge Sharp*, I've changed my life in the following way:

One way this book could have been more helpful to me is: